Strength and Tenacity:

Research on Reputation Building of Chinese State-owned Enterprises in the U.S.

Tian Xiangning

authorHOUSE

AuthorHouse™
1663 Liberty Drive
Bloomington, IN 47403
www.authorhouse.com
Phone: 833-262-8899

Published by AuthorHouse 07/22/2022

ISBN: 978-1-6655-6588-2 (sc)
ISBN: 978-1-6655-6589-9 (e)

Library of Congress Control Number: 2022913588

Print information available on the last page.

Contents

1. Introduction

1.1 Research Background

State-owned enterprises (SOEs) play an irreplaceable role in China's economic structure. In recent years, SOEs have continuously developed overseas, and by the end of 2021, China's SOEs had opened over 10,000 overseas units, covering 185 countries and regions, generating great economic benefit and social influence. Especially under the influence of China's "One Belt, One Road" development strategy, state-owned enterprises have accelerated the layout of overseas business, and a number of enterprises have proposed the "overseas first" development strategy, providing a strong impetus for global economic construction.

In the Fortune 500 list released in 2019, the number of Chinese companies on the list reached 129, of which 48 are state-owned enterprises, and in particular, three of the top five on the list are SOEs. This indicates that the hard power of Chinese SOEs has been recognized worldwide to some extent.

However, despite the international recognition of their economic success, Chinese SOEs do not perform well in the world brand rankings. There are four well-known global brand rankings: the World Brand 500 list released by World Brand Lab, the Top 100 Best

Global Brands list released by Interbrand, the Top 100 Most Valuable Global Brands list released by Millward Brown, and the Top 500 Global Brand Value list released by Brand Finance. In the above four lists in 2019, the number of China's SOEs on the list is 23, 0, 5 and 9, respectively, which clearly shows that the brand recognition of SOEs does not match with their economic strength.

What led to this situation? In terms of the external environment, the international public opinion environment faced by Chinese SOEs has become more and more intricate and complex. Although the number of overseas media reports on Chinese SOEs is increasing, there is a clear ideological bias in the reports. In terms of their own construction, Chinese SOEs' overseas communication capabilities are still insufficient, and they have not established a reasonable and efficient communication strategy.

It can be seen that although SOEs have outstanding performance in the aspect of economic strength, their brand recognition still needs to be improved, which, together with the negative impact of the international public opinion environment, makes the construction of SOEs' overseas reputation face outstanding difficulties.

1.2 Research Objectives and Research Questions

The competitiveness of enterprises is a combination of hard and soft power. Successful companies need to improve their products and technology as well as optimize their image and reputation. Reputation is a unique and irreplaceable asset for companies, and having a sound reputation is not only the basis for sustainable development, but also the key to gaining strategic competitive advantage. At the same time, enterprises are an important carrier of national image, and for Chinese SOEs, building a good international reputation plays a positive role in enhancing and shaping China's national image (Fan, 2013).

Among all the overseas markets explored by Chinese SOEs, the United States is undoubtedly one of the most strategically important target markets. China-U.S. trade is the most important trade relationship in the world, and SOEs' operations in the U.S. are a necessary path to integrate into economic globalization. Meanwhile, China-U.S. trade is also the most complex trade relationship in the world, and the interests of the two countries are deeply intertwined as well as full of games and frictions, which adds uncertainties to the development of SOEs in the U.S. Therefore, the issue of reputation building for SOEs in the U.S. is significant and challenging, and research on the practices of SOEs in the U.S. can provide more inspiration and references for other overseas SOEs.

Based on the above analysis, this study focuses on the U.S. market and examines the reputation building models of two SOEs belonging to the construction and manufacturing industries, respectively. The study summarizes the experiences of different companies and also analyzes the challenges they meet.

This book aims to provide a theoretical basis and practical guidance for the international development of SOEs, and the entire study attempts to address the following questions:

1. From a communication perspective, what are the internal and external factors that influence SOEs' reputation building overseas? What is the relationship between the different factors?

2. Focusing on the U.S. market, how have SOEs in the U.S. combined their communication strategies to build reputation,

what kind of reputation effects have they achieved, and what are their limitations and shortcomings?

3. How should Chinese overseas SOEs further improve their corporate reputation by adjusting their corporate communication strategies?

1.3 Literature Review

1.3.1 Research by International Scholars

In the Scopus database, literature was searched with the keyword "Corporate Reputation". The results show that relevant research has experienced rapid growth in recent decades and can be broadly divided into three phases based on time and volume, as shown in the figure below.

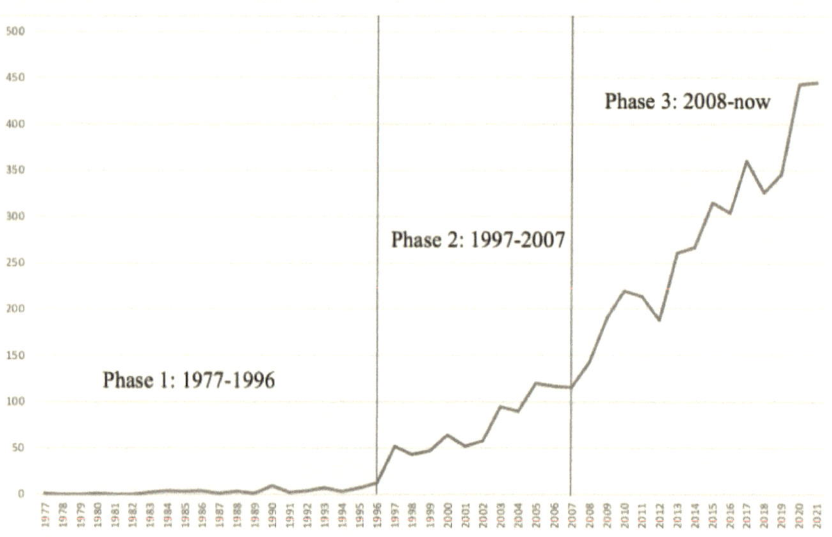

Figure 1.1 Number of Relevant Literature

1.3.1.1 Phase One: Signal/Benefit Research Perspective

Since the 1970s, scholars have begun to research one corporate reputation. Early studies focused on how companies can gain economic returns and competitive advantage through sending signals to the public that show their capabilities. The research in this period was mostly based on signal theory, which refers to the idea that companies send out a series of signals about their finances and quality from which investors and consumers can infer whether they are reliable or not, and use these signals to predict the future behavior of companies.

Weigelt and Camerer (1988) have pointed out that factors such as product quality, leader reputation, and bank credit history can be taken as market signals through which consumers may infer a company's reputation and understand corporate behavior. Fombrun and Shanley (1990) added that in addition to market signals, companies can also release institutional signals to the public that conform to social norms to win public favor as well as reputation.

As can be seen, early studies on corporate reputation focused mainly on the organizational level, with more emphasis on one-way information dissemination, rather than on the interaction between corporate and stakeholders. As for the effect of corporate reputation, signal theory suggests that economic benefits and financial performance should be used as measures.

1.3.1.2 Phase Two: Perception/Relationship Research Perspective

Since the late 1990s, research on corporate reputation has further intensified, and scholars have begun to identify the difference between corporate reputation and other concepts such as corporate identity, corporate image, and brand, in order to better clarify the connotation of corporate reputation.

An increasing number of scholars have begun to regard corporate reputation as the feelings and perceptions of different stakeholders about a company. Fombrun (1997) defines corporate reputation as a perceptual representation of a company's past actions and future prospects that describes the company's overall appeal to all of its key constituents when compared with other leading competitors, which remains one of the most cited definitions in the literature.

During this phase, stakeholder theory was introduced into the study of corporate reputation, and researchers realized the need to value two-way communication between companies and their stakeholders in order to gain reputation (Vendelø, 1998; Davies et al, 2001). Key stakeholders include internal stakeholders, such as employees and shareholders; and external stakeholders, such as suppliers and customers (Campbell & Alexander, 1997). Some scholars also point out that in addition to the above-mentioned interest groups, government, media, and social organizations are also stakeholders of the companies, which means that corporate reputation effects are not only determined by economic benefits but are also influenced by their social performance (Mahon, 2002).

With the introduction of stakeholder theory, public relations scholars have gradually become the main force in reputation research. For example, Hutton (2001) conducted a survey of communications executives at Fortune 500 companies and found that a growing number of respondents were beginning to embrace reputation management as a corporate operating philosophy and apply it to stakeholder relationship management. Gibson (2006) states that PR practitioners can help organizations integrate media resources and communicate with the public, and they are in a unique position to build or repair organizational reputation.

Tools to assess corporate reputation effects also started to emerge at this phase, for instances, after defining reputation as the overall perception of the company by various stakeholders, Fombrun (2000) proposed the famous reputation index model.

In summary, the connotation and extension of corporate reputation have been greatly expanded. On the one hand, the introduction of stakeholder theory has turned corporate reputation into an interactive and developing relationship model, and on the other hand, both business benefits and social performance have become criteria for assessing the corporate reputation effects.

1.3.1.3 Phase Three: Communication/Management Perspective

After the first decade of the 21st century, scholars began to focus on the relationship between communication management activities and corporate reputation. Related research topics include media communication and corporate reputation, corporate social responsibility and reputation, crisis management and reputation, and internal corporate communication and reputation.

In terms of media communication, Carroll and McCombs (2003) bring agenda-setting theory to corporate reputation literature, and explore effects of media on corporate reputation development.

As for social responsibility, a large number of empirical studies have conducted on corporate social responsibility activities and corporate communication activities, and have found that these two variables tend to show a positive correlation with corporate reputation (Nielsen & Thomsen, 2009; Eberle et al, 2013). Dowling and Moran (2012) argue that only by considering corporate responsibility as a foundational element of corporate strategy can companies gain the most significant reputation advantage.

In the field of crisis management, Coombs and other scholars have studied the role of reputation capital in corporate crisis management, and found that a companies's accumulated reputation in the past can generate halo effect that protects the companies during a crisis and makes stakeholders less likely to blame the companies (Coombs & Holladay, 2006; Shim & Yang, 2016).

In case of internal communication, scholars have examined the importance that corporate management places on internal communication and found a significant relationship with corporate reputation (Dortok, 2006), while others have applied identity theory to their research and found that a good corporate reputation can lead to positive professional and organizational identity among employees (Ashforth et al, 2013).

As we can see that corporate reputation research has shifted from the early "signal/benefit" perspective to the "relationship/perception" perspective, and gradually evolved to the "communication/management" perspective. Numerous studies have confirmed the importance of reputation to corporate development and noted the need to build reputation by planning different types of communication activities, which also provides a reference for this study.

Table1.1 Theoretical Perspectives on
Corporate Reputation Research

Perspective	Main theories	Topics
Signal/Benefit	Signal Theory	How companies gain economic benefits by releasing reputation signals

Relationship/ Perception	Stakeholder Theory	How companies enhance their reputation by maintaining relationships with stakeholders
Communication/ Management	Agenda Setting Theory, Social Capital Theory, Identity Theory, etc.	Corporate social responsibility and reputation, crisis management and reputation, internal corporate communication and reputation, etc.

1.3.2 Research by Chinese Scholars

On the website of the National Library of China, the search for Chinese literature with the keyword "corporate reputation" shows that there are 1,725 relevant articles in the past 30 years. Based on time and volume, they can also be divided into three phases, as shown in the figure below.

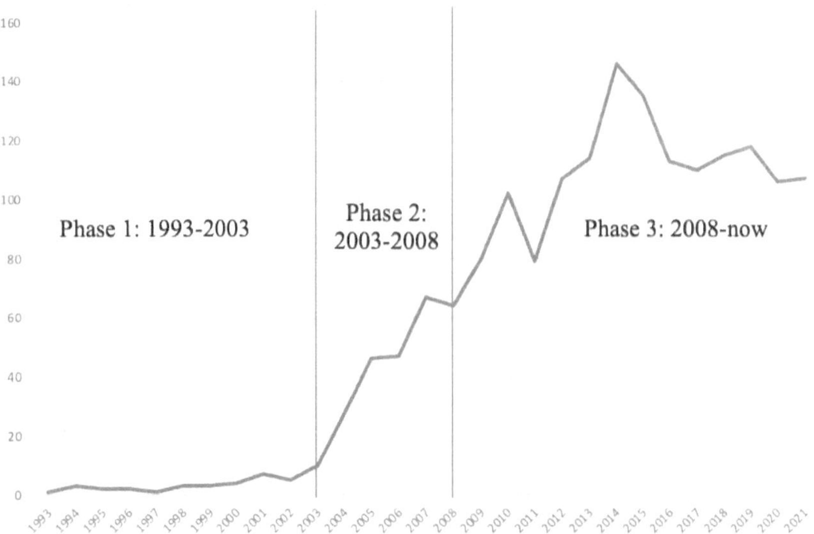

Figure 1.2 Number of Relevant Literature

1.3.2.1 *Phase One: Introduction to the Theory of Corporate Reputation*

Research on corporate reputation in China began in the early 1990s. In the beginning, Chinese scholars' articles on corporate reputation mainly introduced Western theories and explained the importance of reputation. Wang Xinxin (1998), Yu Jinjin (2003), Bai Yongxiu and Xu Hong (2001) are among the pioneer scholars who introduced reputation theory to China. Chinese scholars of this phase were mainly with background in management, and they have explored the connotation and necessity of corporate reputation and clarified the relevant theoretical paths, but little has been said about specific practical measures to build reputation.

1.3.2.2 *Phase Two: Evaluation and Measurement of Corporate Reputation*

China's accession to the WTO in the 21st century has led Chinese companies to face the challenges of globalization, which resulted in a significant increase in the number of studies related to corporate reputation.

During this phase, the evaluation and measurement of corporate reputation has been concerned by Chinese scholars, and some of them tried to explore an evaluation system that meets the Chinese context. Liu Liang (2005) pointed out that corporate reputation can be measured by dividing it into endogenous components and exogenous components, and she conducted an empirical study taking private enterprises in Zhejiang as an example. Based on foreign reputation models, Fang Zheng (2008) proposed a system of indicators for corporate reputation in China, including five primary indicators of product and service quality, financial performance, strategic development, emotion and attraction, and organizational management.

Besides, Chinese scholars have also tried to measure specific reputation influencing factors. Wang Le (2004) constructed a reputation evaluation model for CEOs, which evaluates CEOs' reputation in three dimensions: personal competence, personal character and ethics. Wang Yangcheng (2006) proposed criteria to evaluate talent attractiveness for a company, including several dimensions of corporate strength, corporate characteristics, personnel management and corporate culture.

Compared to previous studies, research at this stage has made considerable progress, but still lacks guidance for company practice. Most scholars came from economics and management discipline, and a small number of scholars came from the field of public relations, while few scholars have conducted studies on corporate reputation from a communication perspective.

1.3.2.3 *Phase Three: Empirical Research on the Factors Influencing Corporate Reputation*

Corporate reputation research in China has grown rapidly since 2008, with scholars analyzing the relationship between reputation and a variety of variables such as corporate social responsibility, consumer loyalty, corporate financial performance, and stakeholder relations.

A few scholars have discussed the role of corporate reputation as a mediating variable in the corporate management process. Li Haiqin and Zhang Zigang (2010) found that corporate reputation is the mediator variable and through CSR works on customer satisfaction. Similarly, Huo Bin and Zhou Haiyan (2014) found that the mediating effect of corporate reputation also acts between CSR and corporate financial performance.

Other scholars have conducted studies on the direct influence of corporate reputation. Li Xin and Peng Huagang (2010) found that the higher the level of CSR information disclosure, the better the reputation they can achieve. Lian Chunhui (2016) found that the release of corporate social responsibility information can change stakeholders' evaluation of the company, further influencing stakeholders' perceptions of corporate reputation.

Overall, Chinese scholars in the aforementioned studies have commonly used well-established scales from Western studies to examine corporate reputation and to test the role played by reputation as a variable. Due to this, these studies have made limited contributions to the theoretical development of corporate reputation.

1.4 Research Methods

This book adopts a combination of quantitative and qualitative research methods, mainly including: Case studies, in-depth interview, and semantic network analysis.

1.4.1 Case Study Method

"A case study is an empirical inquiry that investigates a contemporary phenomenon within its real-life context, especially when the boundaries between phenomenon and context are not clearly evident" (Yin, 2009). Anderson and Arsenault (2005) argue that case studies typically examine the interplay of all variables in order to provide as complete an understanding of an event or situation as possible. Case studies are an ideal method when a comprehensive, in-depth investigation is required (Feagin et al, 1991). Specifically, the process of a case study consists of four steps: designing a research protocol, collecting research data, analyzing research evidence, and making conclusions and recommendations based on the research evidence (Noor, 2008).

In order to better understand the current situation and characteristics of SOEs' reputation building in the U.S., I first reviewed the operation of Chinese SOEs in the U.S. (see table 1.2). As the table shows, SOEs began to enter the U.S. market after China's reform and opening-up. Related enterprises are mainly distributed in the energy and chemical industry, architectural engineering industry, information and communication industry, transportation industry and mechanical manufacture industry.

Table 1.2 China's SOEs Operating in the United States

Time of Entry	Industry Category	Name of the Enterprise
1984	Energy and Chemical	China Petrochemical Corporation
1985	Architectural Engineering	China State Construction Engineering Corporation
1988	Energy and Chemical	China Minmetals Corporation
2000	Transportation	China Shipping Corporation
2001	Architectural Engineering	China National Building Materials Group Corporation
2002	Information and Communication	China Telecom
2003	Information and Communication	China Unicom
2010	Infrastructure Construction	China Communications Construction Company
2015	Mechanical Manufacture	China Railway Rolling Stock Corporation
2015	Transportation	China Railway Engineering Corporation
2011	Mechanical Manufacture	Aviation Industry Corporation of China

I selected the subsidiaries of China State Construction Engineering Corporation and China Railway Rolling Stock Corporation as the subjects of this study, which are China Construction America (CCA) and China Railway Rolling Stock Corporation America (CRRC America). The reasons are as follows:

First, both companies have a certain scale of operation in the U.S. and maintain close interaction with local stakeholders. Second, the two companies belong to the construction and engineering industry and the machinery manufacturing industry, respectively, which are fast-growing and advantageous industries in China and are receiving high attention in the global market. Third, compared with other companies, these two companies have higher media exposure, and I can obtain more second-hand information about them.

1.4.2 In-depth Interview Method

In order to collect data for the study, this book adopts an in-depth interview method to examine the internal logic of the reputation building of the two companies. In 2019 to 2020, I conducted in-depth interviews with the heads of communication and PR departments from two companies.

In-depth interviews consisted of two rounds. The first round was telephone interviews in which I contacted the interviewees by telephone and asked questions based on a prepared interview outline, lasting from one hour to one and a half hours. The second round of interviews was in-person, and I visited the headquarter office of CCA in Jersey City, New Jersey, as well as the plant of CRRC America in Springfield, Massachusetts, during which I asked additional questions to the heads of both companies. I also had unstructured, free-ranging conversations with other employees of both companies to find out what they think and feel about their jobs.

1.4.3 Semantic Network Analysis Method

Semantic network analysis (SNA) is a research method that first came from the discipline of computer science. Scholars believe that two words have a tie in a semantic network if their uses are related, and relations among words are identified by distance, co-occurrence, and frequency (Doerfel, 1998). Clusters of words can show strong intellectual associations in a text corpus (Lievrouw et al, 1987). Unlike the traditional content analysis that use manual coding, SNA can, to a certain extent, avoid the subjective bias of coders, which is more suitable for text research with larger data size.

Although the SNA method has above advantages, the semantic structure objectively presented by the software still needs to be analyzed and explained by human beings. In previous studies, scholars often use frame theory to interpret computer-mined data. The sociologist Erving Goffman, understood the idea of the frame to mean the culturally determined definitions of reality that allow people to make sense of objects and events (Goffman, 1974). Reese (2007) adds: "framing's value does not hinge on its potential as a unified research domain but as a provocative model that bridges parts of the field that need to be in touch with each other: quantitative and qualitative, empirical and interpretive, psychological and sociological, and academic and professional".

This book collected English-language coverage of the two companies from the U.S. media over a five-year period from the Factiva news database, and used WORDij 3.0 software to analyze the media texts for frequency and co-occurrence, then imports the results into Gephi 0.9.2 software for modularity clustering. As for important semantic clusters, the book conducted frame analysis on them to explore the media coverage characteristics.

1.5 Structure of the Book

This book is structured into seven chapters. The introductive section explains the reputation dilemma faced by Chinese SOEs and presents the research questions of this paper in this context. It reviews the history and trends of reputation research, presents the objectives and methodologies of this study. The first part concludes with an overview of the book structure.

The second chapter focuses on the core concepts and theoretical foundations. It defines the concepts of corporate reputation and corporate communication, and introduces the total corporate communications notion to explain the interaction between different communication activities and corporate reputation. It aims to delimit the scope of work and generates a common understanding of the subjects. The section provides a basis of information for the following chapters.

The third to fifth chapters are the case study part of this book. The third chapter analyzes the external environmental factors affecting reputation building of SOEs, including regulative, normative, and cognitive elements. In the fourth and fifth chapters, the book introduces the reputation building practices of China Construction America (CCA) and China Railway Rolling Stock Corporation America (CRRC America).

The sixth and seventh chapters are the conclusion and discussion. This section proposes an integrated model of overseas reputation building for Chinese SOEs and presents practical suggestions based on it. In addition, it concludes with an outlook on future requirements and potential developments of the subject.

2. Core Concepts and Theoretical Basis

2.1 Corporate Reputation and Corporate Communications

Corporate reputation and corporate communication are concepts that emerged along with the development of corporate business practices. This section defines each of the two concepts and explores the interaction between them.

2.1.1 Definition of Corporate Reputation

2.1.1.1 What is Corporate Reputation?

As early as the 18th century, Adam Smith already recognized the value of reputation as an important mechanism to ensure the successful implementation of business contracts. In the 1860s, "corporate reputation" emerged as an academic concept. According to Levitt (1967), corporate reputation is a combination of consumer perceptions of a company's popularity, trustworthiness and reliability.

Fombrun and Van Riel (1997) reviewed literatures in different disciplines and proposed six views on the connotation of corporate reputation. In the economic viewpoint, reputation is a trait or signal. To strategists, reputations are both assets and mobility barriers. In marketing research reputation focuses on the nature of information processing, resulting in "pictures in the heads". To organizational scholars, corporate reputations are rooted in the sense-making experiences of employees. Organizational sociologists point out that reputation is social constructions that come into being through the relationships that a company has with its stakeholders in a shared institutional environment. From an accounting perspective, reputation is intangible assets that can enhance the value of a company's investment.

The above views reflect various qualities of corporate reputation, on the basis of which Fombrun and Rindova provide an integrated definition of what corporate reputation is: A corporate reputation is a collective representation of a company's past actions and results that describes the company's ability to deliver valued outcomes to multiple stakeholders. It gauges a company's relative standing both internally with employees and externally with its stakeholders, in both its competitive and institutional environments.

In addition to this, other scholars have provided definitions of corporate reputation from different aspects.

First, from a "behavior-result" logic, some scholars view reputation as the influence and result that a company exerts on others through its own behavior. They argue that corporate reputation is inferred from the economic and non-economic behavior of companies (Yoon et al., 1993; Weigelt & Camerer, 1988). Melewar (2008) states that the economic factors that affect corporate reputation include product and service quality, competence and technology, performance and financial performance, while non-economic factors include corporate social responsibility, media exposure and media relations.

Second, some scholars are more concerned about the relationship between corporate reputation and stakeholders. Wartick (1992) suggested that corporate reputation is the sum of multiple stakeholders' perceptions of the companies. Saxon (1998) and Whetten (2002) also point out that stakeholders tend to use their own expectations of the companies as a criterion to examine the companies, and the companies can only gain reputation if it can meet the expectations of different stakeholders. Gotsi and Wilson (2001) argue that reputation is the overall evaluation of a company made by stakeholders over a long period of time.

Third, other scholars define corporate reputation in terms of attitude structure. Hall (1992) argues that reputation is an attitudinal structure composed of perceptions and emotions. Manfred (2004) divided corporate reputation into two dimensions: rational cognitive and emotional experience, which include people's both objective judgments and subjective emotional experiences of the company. In 2008, Swiss scholars Imhof and Eisenegger included the normative dimension in their definition of corporate reputation and claimed that it is a value rationality between cognition and emotion.

Based on the above definitions, this book argues that corporate reputation is a collective perception by stakeholders of a company's past behavior and future prospects, and this perception is the result of the interaction of cognition, emotion and moral norm.

2.1.1.2 Comparison of Corporate Reputation with Other Concepts

Corporate identity, corporate image, corporate brand and corporate reputation are four dominant concepts involved in the process of corporate communication. To better identify corporate reputation with other related concepts, this book provides a comparison of them.

Identity refers to the set of qualities and beliefs that make one person or group different from others (Somers, 1994). Like individuals, organizations can be viewed as subsuming a multiplicity of identities, each of which is appropriate for a given context or audience (Balmer & Greyser, 2002). Companies can identify themselves and distinguish themselves from other companies at multiple levels, thereby expressing corporate values and forming reliable stakeholder relationships (Melewar, 2003).

Corporate identity is characteristics of a company's self-perception, addressing the question of "who we are", while corporate reputation is a collection of perceptions held by stakeholders, addressing the question of "how others perceive us". Companies can create their own identity through internal strategic planning, philosophical positioning and culture creating, while corporate reputation building involves considering the needs of all internal and external stakeholders (Balmer, 1994). In short, corporate identity emphasizes the self-positioning of a company, whereas corporate reputation emphasizes the collective perception by all stakeholders which needs to be built and maintained by all members of the company.

Most definitions of image focus on "the feelings and beliefs about the company that exist in the minds of its audiences" (Bernstein 1992). Another way of interpreting image is "what comes to mind when one hears the name or sees the logo" (Gray & Balmer 1998). If corporate image is the "mental interpretation" of an organization then it will be affected by external factors in people's perceptions (e.g., media, competitor strategies, individual preferences) but this does not stop it being shaped and deliberately managed by the organization through its marketing and communications (Wartick, 1992; Cramer & Ruefli, 1994). The marketing and organizational approaches to understanding image can be combined, as described by Alvesson and Willmott (1990) in their conclusion that: "corporate image is a holistic and vivid impression held by an individual or a particular group towards a company and is a result of sense-making by the group and communication by the company of a fabricated and projected picture of itself."

Although image and reputation both refer to external perceptions and the views of stakeholders, there is a key distinction between the concepts. Thus, image relates to someone's current and latest beliefs about an organization rather than the longer-term perspective involved in reputation, which relates to the interpretation of organizational behavior over a period of time (Chun 2005; Fillis 2003). It is therefore possible to have an image of an organization without having any direct experience of it, whereas reputation implies a foundation in experience (Chun 2005). Consequently, reputation is also more durable than image and can act as a positive store of goodwill and support or a negative bank of distrust and avoidance (Melewar 2003). A company can have a good reputation yet possess an old-fashioned or otherwise inappropriate image; or, conversely, a company can have a strong image developed through its visual identity and marketing program, which is not matched by a cogent reputation (Bennett & Gabriel 2003). Thus, an image may be good for immediate and short-term decisions, while reputation is useful for long-term decisions (Bennett & Gabriel 2003).

As for corporate brand, marketing scholars argue that companies can build strong brands through marketing activities to influence stakeholders' assessment of corporate reputation (Hatch & Schultz, 2008; Hatch & Schultz, 2001). The difference between corporate reputation and corporate brand is that corporate brand is closely related to a company's sales behavior, weak brands are less attractive to consumers, while strong brands are more attractive, and brands influence the likelihood that consumers make purchasing decisions. Reputation, on the other hand, is about all the behaviors of the company, so it can be said that brand management is a subset of reputation management (Fomburn & van Riel, 2004).

As we can see from the range of definitions described above, there are two main dimensions to understand the relationship between corporate identity, corporate image, corporate brand and corporate reputation.

From the perspective of problem solving, the core problems to be solved by these concepts are different (Brown et al, 2006). Corporate identity answers the question "Who are we as a company?" Corporate intended image answers the question "What does the company want others to think about the company?" Corporate constructed image answers the question "What does the company believe others think of the company?" Corporate reputation answers the question "What do stakeholders actually think of the company?"

In terms of time period, as mentioned above, corporate identity is the long-term identification feature established and maintained by the company, corporate image is the impression of the company obtained by stakeholders in a relatively short period of time, and corporate brand and corporate Reputation is the result of being shaped over a long period of time.

Table 2.1 Dimensions of Corporate Identity,
Image, Brand and Reputation

Dimensions	Corporate Identity	Corporate Intended Image	Corporate Constructed Image	Corporate Brand	Corporate Reputation
Viewpoint	Who are we as a company?	What does the company want others to think about the company?	What does the company believe others think of the company?	What does the company want others to think about the company?	What do stakeholders actually think of the company?
Time period	Long-term	Short-term	Short-term	Long-term	Long-term

2.1.2 Definition of Corporate Communication

Corporate communications, similar to corporate reputation, is a multidisciplinary crossroads. In the early days, scholars and practitioners used the term "public relations" to refer to the communication activities of companies with all stakeholders. Since the 1960s, some U.S. companies began to establish departments dedicated to corporate communications (Ihator, 2004), and by the 1980s, corporate communications became a specialized field of study.

David Bernstein, considered a pioneer in the field of corporate communication research (Balmer & Greyser, 2009), pointed out that communication is a resource that is generally underestimated by companies (Bernstein, 1984). With the development of theory and practice, the number of researchers in corporate communication has gradually increased. There are three distinct perspectives on how the corporate communication concept should be defined and explored.

The strategic management lens regards corporate communication as a managerial way of thinking that involves managing and orchestrating all the internal and external activities of a company, and integrating advertising, PR, crisis management, and public affairs (Christensen, 2002; Argenti et al, 2005; Van Riel & Fombrun, 2007). Consequently, companies need to take a strategic approach to conducting communication activities so that key stakeholders can understand and agree on corporate behavior, thereby building an operating environment conducive to long-term growth.

The second paradigm embracing the stakeholder perspective. Corporate communication is viewed as the two-way exchange of information with different stakeholders through different forms of communication. Goodman (1994) states that corporate communication is the communication behavior of a companies based on its characteristics and its relationships with suppliers, communities, employees and customers. Gray and Balmer (1998) believe that corporate communication is the process by which companies communicate formal and informal information to various stakeholders through different media channels.

The final component of the troika of perspectives, seeks to disclose that all corporate communication activities have clear purpose. As Jackson (1987) observes, corporate communication is the sum of communication activities carried out by a company to achieve its goals. For example, short-term marketing communication activities are aimed at selling products and services, internal management communication is aimed at achieving corporate consensus, and external public relations is aimed at maintaining good relations with various stakeholders. The scholars, while recognizing the above difference, generally agree with the view that the ultimate goal of corporate communication is to shape and maintain corporate reputation. According to Cornelissen (2011), the ultimate goal of corporate communication is to coordinate all communication objectives, targets and channels to achieve corporate reputation.

Based on the above viewpoints, this book argues that corporate communication is a management function that aims to achieve corporate goals and provides a framework for effective coordination with all stakeholders.

2.1.3 Total Corporate Communications Notion and Corporate Reputation

Corporate communication is the important way to achieve corporate goals, which include constructing corporate identity, creating a unique corporate image, building a strong corporate brand, and accumulating corporate reputation capital (Dowling & Staelin, 1994; Fombrun & Rindova, 1996). Among all the goals, numerous scholars confirm and emphasize the unique position of corporate reputation as the ultimate goal of corporate communication. Van Riel and Fombrun (2007) highlight that creating a good reputation should be top requisites on the company's development growth list and not kept in isolation and therefore, reputation is considered one of the most crucial strategic resources the companies can have.

Scholars have generally acknowledged the role of corporate communications in contributing to reputation building and are continuously exploring specific mechanisms of influence, with scholar Balmer (1999, 2017), an important founder of this research area, proposing the total corporate communications notion.

This book introduces Balmer's total corporate communications notion to further understand the relationship between corporate communications and reputation. The notion holds that everything a company says, makes and does — as well as what others say about a company communicates, thereby companies should try to coordinate all communication activities in order to achieve the goal of reputation (Balmer, 1995). Specifically, Balmer divides corporate communication into three levels.

The primary communication is the substantive behavior of the company, including its management approach, products and services, and marketing activities. The secondary communication is formal corporate communication in the traditional sense, that is, purposeful corporate communication activities. The tertiary communication is information about the company produced by third parties not controlled by the company, and media coverage is the main representative of this type of communication activity.

While academic discussions on corporate communication usually stay at the second level, which focuses on how companies use controllable channels to communicate with stakeholders, total corporate communications notion takes into account corporate behavior and external public opinion as important forms of communication that affect corporate reputation. Stuart (1999) argues that total corporate communications is a notion that is more comprehensive and accord with the interdisciplinary nature of corporate communication.

Based on the total corporate communications notion, this book argues that corporate reputation is affected by a three-part system process with the corporate behavior as primary communication, the formal communication strategy as secondary communication, and the media opinion as tertiary communication. Primary communication can accumulate signals about the company's reputation through substantial activities, and these signals need to be delivered to stakeholders with the help of secondary communication, in which uncontrollable noise plays the role of tertiary communication (see figure 2.1).

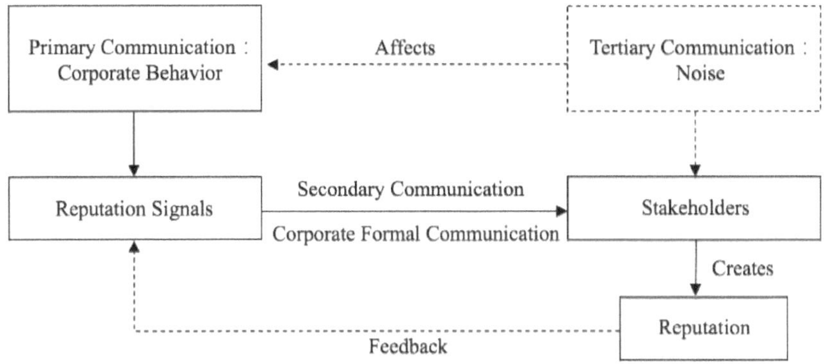

Figure 2.1 Total Corporate Communications and Reputation

On the one hand, companies should establish their own goals and missions and carry out reputation building behaviors to accumulate reputation signals. On the other hand, companies need to make their stakeholders understand and recognize their reputation building behaviors through specific communication strategies. At the same time, companies also need to intervene the tertiary communication appropriately to reduce the impact of external noise.

2.2 Elements Affecting the Corporate Reputation Building

2.2.1 Primary Communication: Corporate Reputation Building Behavior

As discussed above, companies can create reputation signals through reputation building behavior. In order to better examine reputation building behavior, this book proposes three dimensions of reputation composition, dividing corporate behavior into three types: identity positioning, competence building, and ethics establishing.

This approach is based on the observation that rationalization of modern thinking has led to a differentiation into three worlds in which all actors have to prove themselves: these are the subjective, the objective and the social worlds (Habermas, 1988). Each of these three worldviews is characterized by a specific rationality of action and appraisal that determines the logic of reputation constitution. In the subjective world, interest focuses on the kind of emotional impact made by the individual character of the agents. In the objective world, the agents are judged on whether they serve the purposes and tasks they have been set in a way capable of cognitive verification. In the social world, finally, ethical correctness is the criterion of judgement (Imhof & Eisenegger, 2008).

This book argues that the composition of corporate reputation also needs to follow the logic of the three worlds, in which reputation is built in the subjective, objective and social worlds. Reputation building in the subjective world is the company's identity positioning, reputation building in the objective world is the company's competence building, and reputation building in the social world is the company's ethics establishing.

Corporate identity is a company's self-perception in the subjective world and, as analyzed in the literature review, answers the question of "who we are". Identity is an enduring, distinctive, and central statement perceived by a company's members (Albert & Whetten, 1985). Numerous scholars agree that identity positioning is the first step in creating corporate reputation (Foreman & Argenti, 2005; Gray and Balmer, 1998). To position a company's identity, it is necessary for the company to identify its core values and uniqueness, and to maintain and preserve them over time. A company's identity involves its vision, mission, values, overall strategy, and management approaches, which are often difficult to measure (Melewar, 2003; Melewar & Karaosmanoglu, 2006). Only when all members of the company are clear about "who we are" can they know how to make strategic decisions and choose the right communication approach to maintain relationships with stakeholders (Tripsas, 2009).

Corporate competence is the sum of elements that enable a company to gain competitive advantage in the objective world. Unlike corporate identity, corporate competence follows a logic of facts, it can be measured by objective figures and facts, including product sales and financial performance. Companies are the main body that creates value in the market, and achieving financial goals is the fundamental task of corporate operation. Companies need to build their competitive advantages in the objective market through continuous competence building, which is the basic precondition for companies to build reputation.

Corporate ethics is about how companies prove themselves in a world full of ethical standards and normative constraints. Corporate ethics is about how companies prove themselves in a world full of ethical standards and normative constraints. Numerous studies reveal that good ethical performance can positively influence business performance, and that honest corporate behavior and responsible corporate attitudes are necessary attributes for modern companies (Kaptein & Van Dalen, 2000; Joyner and Payne, 2002). In the social world, on the one hand, companies need to ensure compliant operations and let employees fulfill professional codes of conduct (Weaver et al, 1999); On the other hand, companies need to contribute to society through voluntary ethical activities and integrate social responsibility into their strategy and culture (Friedma, 2007; Fan, 2009).

The reputation building behaviors of companies in the above three dimensions are mutually reinforcing and complementary. A well-developed corporate identity can guide a company's ethical activities. Employees' perception of corporate ethics in turn influences their corporate identity. While sound corporate competence is the fundamental economic guarantee of all behaviors.

Table 2.2 Corporate Reputation Building Behaviors

Dimension	Purpose	Main Content	Source of Theory
Identity Positioning (Subjective World)	Create the uniqueness and attractiveness of the company.	Corporate vision, mission, value and management approach	T. Melewar, 2003; Foreman & Argenti, 2005; Gray & Balmer, 1998
Competence Building (Objective World)	Gain objective competitive advantages.	Financial performance, product and service quality	Eberl & Schwaiger, 2005
Ethics Establishing (social World)	Achieve business legitimacy and ethical recognition.	Corporate compliance, charitable activities, community volunteerism, and socially responsible business practices	Solomon, 1992; Carroll, 1998; Kotler & Lee, 2008

2.2.2 Secondary Communication: Corporate Communication Strategy

In order to deliver reputation signals to stakeholders, companies need to use secondary communication, which is the traditional corporate communication strategy. This book believes that corporate communication strategy consists of three parts: communication objectives, communication functions and communication skills.

Although the ultimate goal of corporate communication is reputation building, it also includes short-term and medium-term goals according to the length of time. The short-term goal of corporate communication is to increase the sales performance; the medium-term goal of corporate communication is to improve corporate image; and the long-term goal of corporate communication is to create a positive environment for the company, so as to promote the formation of corporate reputation (Mahoney, 2013; Hu et al., 2019).

The corporate communication function refers to the role of communications department in the company. Grunig (2003) believes that the position of the communications department in an organization is divided into two types: the center and the periphery. The former means that the organization integrates the communications department into corporate strategy, while the latter means that the communications department is not able to participate in the top-level decisions of the company. According to Dozier (1992), communication practitioners have two dominant roles in an organization: technician role and the managerial role. The technician is seen as someone who produces, for example, brochures, pamphlets, and so on. In other words, they perform the various task-related or operational aspects of public relations. The managerial role is empowered as decision-makers at the strategic level.

Companies should choose the appropriate forms of communication according to different communication objectives. This book considers that corporate communication covers three types which are internal communication, marketing communication and public relations. Internal communication are communication activities within a company that aim to make employees believe in the company's values, and improve their organizational identification (Pincus et al, 1991). Marketing communication is the communication activities carried out to sell goods and services, such as advertising and promotion, and customers are the main target of marketing communication. Public relations includes government relations, community relations, media relations, and other forms of communication (Grunig, 1992).

In summary, companies need to implement strategies according to their internal and external conditions, which will present different characteristics of communication strategies.

2.2.3 Tertiary Communication: Impact of Media Coverage

The total corporate communications approach views uncontrollable noise as tertiary communication that affects reputation building. No matter how hard a company tries to perceive its reputation through its actions and expressions, the perceptions of stakeholders are still influenced by a variety of intermediaries (Rindova, 1997). Institutional intermediaries facilitate the formation of impressions and evaluations of companies. They specialize in the collection and transmission of information and accumulate resources and expertise to do so a lot more effectively than more constituents can do on their own. Because of their role, intermediaries become central nodes in interorganizational networks, which increases their access to information.

The media is the most important intermediary in the process of corporate reputation building. Fombrun and Shanley (1990) view media coverage as a potential prerequisite for corporate reputation. In later research, Fombrun (1995) argues that since people rarely have direct personal experience with companies, they usually learn about companies through the coverage of journalists, who filter and present information about companies.

Craig Carroll focuses on the impact of media coverage on corporate reputation based on agenda-setting theory. He examined the first-level agenda setting and second-level agenda setting of the media for companies and found that the media agenda has a significant impact on the public agenda, i.e., "The media determines which companies to think about" and "The media determines how to think about these companies" (Carroll, 2004).

This impact is even more significant in two cases. One is that national media are most effective in promoting the agenda, with the Wall Street Journal is proved to play a dominant role in public opinion on business topics (Ragas and Roberts, 2009). The other one is that the less direct experience stakeholders have with the company, the more they will rely on media coverage to reduce information uncertainty (Einwiller et al, 2010).

In conclusion, media coverage plays an important role in the formation of corporate reputation. Especially for the SOEs studied in this book, the public has less direct personal experience with SOEs and relies more on media reports to obtain information about them, which makes the influence of media on public opinion more significant.

2.2.4 The Institutional Environment for Company

There is no company that operates in a vacuum, and the external environment plays a crucial role in the process of corporate reputation building. Especially for multinational companies, they must be embedded in the institutional environment of the country in which they operate.

Institutions include both formal rules, which are explicit, written rules such as laws and constitutions, and informal constraints such as conventions and norms. Organizational sociologist Scott was the first to include institutional elements in the study of corporate strategy (Wu, 2011). Regulative, normative, and cognitive social systems have all been identified by theorists as central elements of institutions (Scott, 1995). These three elements constitute the institutional environment in which multinational companies operate.

Table 2.3 exemplifies some of the key dimensions along which these elements differ.

Table 2.3 Regulative, Normative, and Cognitive Elements of Institutions

Dimension	Regulative	Normative	Cognitive
Legitimacy	Legal systems	Moral and ethical systems	Cultural systems
Central Rudiments	Policies and rules	Work roles, habits and norms	Values, beliefs and assumptions
System Drivers	Legal obligation	Moral obligation	Internalized values
Behavioral Reasoning	Have to	Ought to	Want to

Regulative institutions consist of policies, laws, and rules made by state authorities. For multinational companies, regulative institutions include both the domestic laws and regulations and the foreign political and economic policies of the host country. A good international bilateral relationship between a company's home and host countries usually makes the business operation across borders smoother, and vice versa increases the obstacles for the company.

Normative institutions are social expectations for companies to fulfill their responsibilities and ethical obligations, and they are not mandatory measures. If regulative institutions are written contracts, normative institutions are more like psychological contracts. In different host countries, stakeholders have different ethical expectations and pressures on companies, and they also have different preferences for corporate responsibility.

Cognitive institutions are the values, beliefs, and assumptions shared by a society, including the thinking, feeling, and behavior patterns of its members. For multinational firms, the greater the distinction between the cognitive institutions of their host and home countries, the more pronounced the challenges to reputation building (Kogut & Singh, 1988).

The three elements mentioned above jointly constitute the institutional environment of a country, and such institutional environment also affects the way multinational companies behave.

3. The Institutional Environment Affecting Corporate Reputation Building for Chinese SOEs in the U.S.

In the process of reputation building, multinational companies are influenced by the institutional environment of the host country in various ways. This chapter presents the regulative, normative, and cognitive institutional environments of the U.S. and examines how these elements impact on the reputation building of Chinese SOEs in the U.S.

3.1 Regulative Institutional Environment: Structural Influence of Political Pressure

Global compliance is the process of a business following all laws, rules, standards, and regulations that apply to them across the globe. Fulfillment of U.S. legal regulations is essential to the operation of Chinese SOEs. In addition, the complex bilateral relationship between the U.S. and China sets unique barriers for Chinese companies in the U.S.

Since the 21ˢᵗ century, the relationship between China and the U.S. has gone through complex changes (He & Xu, 2019). Around 2013, the U.S. gradually transferred its strategic emphasis from the Middle East to the Asia–Pacific, and began to regard China as one of the most important external threats (Cao & Wang, 2018).

In 2018, the U.S. government defined China as "rival" and "adversary" in the National Security Strategy Report and the National Defense Strategy Report, which is the most severe strategic positioning of the U.S. towards other countries since the Cold War. It is clear that the U.S. policy toward China has become competition-oriented, and this strategy is quickly affecting the operations of Chinese companies.

As China's economic influence expanded, the U.S. government began implementing a series of coercive measures to exclude Chinese companies from U.S. industries. The U.S.-China trade war officially kicked off in April 2018 when the Office of the U.S. Trade Representative announced a 25% tariff hike on a number of Chinese imports. In addition to imposing tariffs, the U.S. is trying to "decouple" from China. In August 2018, the U.S. Congress signed the Export Control Reform Act, which focuses on the control of key technologies critical to U.S. national security, and the subsequently released control list of emerging technologies, covering biotechnology, artificial intelligence, chip microprocessors, precision navigation, and other technologies, has notable overlaps with the key innovation areas proposed in "Made in China 2025" (Wu, 2019). These actions not only hit Chinese companies, but also cause a huge impact on the global supply chain and disrupt the world economic situation.

At the same time, the U.S. continues to strengthen security reviews of Chinese investments on "national security" grounds. The

Committee on Foreign Investment in the United States (CFIUS) has recommended to Congress that Chinese SOEs should be prohibited from acquiring the assets of U.S. companies, because they could potentially threaten U.S. national security.

Clearly, changes in U.S. policy toward China have had a structural impact on the business environment for Chinese SOEs in the U.S. The regulative institutional environment not only affect direct investment by Chinese companies, but also, to varying degrees, influence the U.S. public's perception of Chinese companies through media coverage.

3.2 Normative Institutional Environment: Ethical Expectations for Companies

At different stages of its history, American society had different perceptions of the social role that companies should assume. In the 1930's, it was commonly believed that shareholders should be the primary beneficiaries of corporate interests and therefore companies were not accountable for the public interest (Berle Jr, 1930). It was in the 1960's when the academic literature acknowledged the relevance of the relationship between corporations and society (Davis, 1960; Frederick, 1960), yet, this perspective remained limited to concerns of employee satisfaction, management and the social welfare of the community and focused mainly on the generation of economic profit. The 1980's were influenced by the social momentum of the time in which there was a growing sense of awareness with regards to the environment and human and labor rights which led to higher social expectations of corporate behavior. As a result, authors pointed out that corporations should assume their obligations as moral subjects (Beauchamp & Bowie, 1980), and the notion of corporate citizenship became widespread in the U.S., where companies were expected to act as social citizens to assume broader social responsibilities than before (Tian, 2005).

The U.S. has a highly developed civil society, with NGOs being an important force in urging companies to take on ethical obligations. On the one hand, NGOs play the role of "pressure groups". Trade unions, industry associations, consumer associations, and environmental organizations representing the rights and interests of different stakeholders will exert pressure on companies through making moral claims. On the other hand, NGOs also play the role of "platform providers". There are about 1.5 million NGOs in the U.S. today, including a large number of public charity organizations and volunteer associations, which provide diverse channels and platforms for companies to fulfill their responsibilities (Ye & He, 2016).

In short, American society expects voluntary, autonomous and broadly engaged civic spirit from companies. Although such an ethical expectation does not exist in legal terms, being a good corporate citizen has become a common consensus among U.S. companies, which has proven to be the most sustainable path for business development in the U.S. market. Since obtaining ethical recognition is an important dimension of corporate reputation building, Chinese SOEs in the U.S. should be more active in fulfilling their responsibilities and building social contracts with their stakeholders to accumulate reputation capital.

3.3 Cognitive Institutional Environment: Cultural Effects of Neoliberalism

The cultural-cognitive dimension reflects the cognitive structures and social knowledge shared by the people in a given country or region. The cognitive elements of institutions are shared conceptions that constitute the nature of reality and the frames through which meaning is made (Scott 2001).

Studies by Hofstede (2001) has revealed that, national culture has effect on the activities of organizational culture—such that, national cultural norms, values and beliefs are forced on organizations through societal establishment (Dennis et al., 2007; Fitzsimmons & Stamper, 2014). Multinational businesses are often confronted with collapse and difficulties which are attributed to insufficient indulgent of the cultural circumstances other than market conditions (Adler, 1991; Lu, Plewa & Ho, 2016).

The American national culture is recognized as being individualistic, freedom-oriented, and competitive (Cook, 2012). These cultural characteristics have also influenced the American political and economic system, such as the emphasis on political equality and the advocacy of free competitive market economy (Deng & Ying, 2012). In particular, since the 1980s, neoliberalism has become the dominant governing ideology of the U.S. government. The U.S. government reduced the proportion of state-owned economy in the national economy, decreased the state's intervention in enterprises, and strongly advocated free competition in the whole market. The neoliberal ideology also influences the values of American society, with the American people generally approving of the jungle law of free competition and being hostile to state-dominated economic forces (Zhang & Wu, 2018), which clearly affects the establishment of identity legitimacy of Chinese SOEs in the United States.

Under the cultural effects of neoliberalism, American society generally views SOEs as inefficient and monopolistic. Such an attitude would contribute to the stereotypical image of Chinese SOEs among the American public.

3.4 Summary

Through an analysis of the U.S. institutional environment, this chapter has found that the reputation building of Chinese SOEs in the U.S. faces external macro-challenges.

The growing conflict of interest between the U.S. and China has led to an increasingly significant influence of political factors in U.S.-China trade, with the U.S. government viewing China and its economic power as "rival" and "threat" by adjusting its strategic positioning and trade policies. U.S. political pressure not only limits investment by Chinese SOEs, but also has a structural impact on the public opinion environment in which they operate, thereby setting a filter on public perceptions of SOEs.

American society advocates free competition and is vigilant about government intervention, which has led to a bias against the economic role of Chinese SOEs, arguing that SOEs do not compete fairly with the U.S. private sector.

Furthermore, there is an increased role for civil society in the U.S., which requires companies to become social citizens for the good of society. In such a normative institutional environment, Chinese SOEs in the U.S. need to place more priority to their social mission, establish contractual relationships with different interest groups, and dissipate the prejudices of U.S. society by increasing their local contributions so that they can maintain their moral legitimacy.

In the next two histories, the book presents case studies of two Chinese SOEs in the U.S., China Construction America and China Railway Rolling Stock Corporation America, examining the specific impact of different institutional environment elements on the reputation building of them and summarizing their response strategies to external challenges.

4. Reputation Building Strategy of China Construction America

Managers are generally confronted with questions of organizational "identity" and "identification"– questions that require addressing "who we are", "what we stand for", "what is our core purpose?", and "what does it mean to be involved in this company?"

Van Riel and Fombrun, 2007

As one of the first Chinese state-owned enterprises to go abroad, China State Construction Engineering Corporation (CSCEC) established China Construction America (CCA) in 1985 and is now firmly rooted in the United States, with approximately 3500 employees and 98% of them are local hires. This section analyzes CCA's reputation building strategy from the perspective of total corporate communications.

4.1 CCA's Reputation Building Behaviors

4.1.1 Corporate Identity Positioning: A Global Company with Local Roots

As mentioned above, a clear corporate identity is the first step in constructing a strong corporate reputation. For multinational companies, the identity of overseas subsidiaries should be positioned on the basis of the vision and mission of the group headquarters, and adjusted according to the business environment of the host country. This book reveals that CCA has localized its corporate values, management style and brand structure, positioning the company as "a global company with local roots".

4.1.1.1 Top-level Design of Mission, Vision and Core Values

Clarifying corporate vision, setting corporate goals, and formulating corporate strategies are prerequisites for corporate development and influence the future orientation of a company (O'Brien & Meadows, 2000; Brown et al, 2006).

CSCEC was one of the first companies in China to implement a systematic branding strategy, and has continuously adjusted its strategic positioning according to the development of the company. As early as 1996, CSCEC has released a corporate image standard manual, which standardizes the corporate logo, office design and even the dress code of employees, ensuring a standard output of corporate image. In 2004, CSCEC refined seven corporate philosophies through internal discussions to clarify the mission, vision, core values and management policy of the company. In 2012, CSCEC upgraded its corporate vision to "become the investment and construction group with the most international competitiveness."

Based on the core principles of the head office, CCA has adapted its own corporate philosophy to the U.S. business environment. As a subsidiary company, their goal is to be the leading construction company in the U.S., which echoes the vision of the head office of becoming a world-class construction group. The head office gives them a large management space to build their corporate culture according to the American society.

Therefore, based on its current business situation and development potential, CCA has positioned its corporate vision as "the most competitive investment and construction group in the Americas" and refined its values as "diligence, teamwork, integrity, innovation and contribution to the community", which emphasizes the quality characteristics cherished by the Eastern society and meets the ethical expectations of the Western society.

4.1.1.2 Adhere to the Localized Management

As the only Chinese construction company incorporated in the U.S., CCA has actively adapted to the local U.S. environment in terms of organizational structure design and management style.

As mentioned in the analysis of the U.S. institutional environment, individualism is a prominent feature of American culture, and Americans respect entrepreneurs and admire corporate heroes (Ding, 2017). With regard to this characteristic, CCA has shown a certain adaptability. CCA values the influence of its company leaders. Unlike most SOEs that use a tenure system for their leadership team, CCA's leadership team has long-term working experience in the United States and understands the American culture well. The current leadership team has been in place since 2000, ensuring the stability of internal management and policy continuity for over 20 years.

In addition, CCA insists on the localization of human resources management, refers to local adaptation where MNCs adapts HRM practices to host country's local firms' practices, i.e., hire local employees in local markets (Bhanugopan and Fish, 2007).

With approximately 3500 employees and 98% of them are local hires, CCA takes a number of measures to guarantee localized operations. Taking full consideration of the low power distance characteristic of American society, CCA provides uniform compensation and equal promotion opportunities for all employees as a way to create an equal organizational atmosphere, in which local employees can compete through internal recruitment to become executives of new projects.

Moreover, CCA has proposed an Employee Training and Development Program to encourage and fund employees to pursue continuing education and self-improvement. As an American company incorporated in the U.S., they don't deny that they have Chinese capital behind, which guarantees the stability of their operations. Furthermore, both for their customers and for their employees, they are trying to make them feel that CCA is no different from an American company, and that they are both serving the American market.

4.1.1.3 Re-branding the Acquired Local Company

In 2014, CCA acquired PLAZA Construction, a New York-based construction company. This acquisition marks a significant step forward in CSCEC's international expansion. It is conducive to increasing the group's market share in developed countries as well as sharpening its competitiveness by becoming more specialized and globalized.

Upon completion of the acquisition, CCA retained PLAZA Construction's original operating team to maintain stability. After a period of management adaptation and integration, CCA rebranded PLAZA Construction. Considering that PLAZA Construction had already accumulated a certain brand awareness in the US, CCA retained its original logo and added the blue logo of CSCEC. Such a rebranding strategy not only ensures the independence of the original local brand, but also highlights the capital dividend and global resource advantages of CCA, and is more convincing to the customers of high-end real estate construction.

CCA never deliberately hide their Chinese SOE background and even consider it as their strength because clients can reap global dividends from it. For the acquired overseas brands, CCA rebrand them to increase their group's brand visibility, which let the main brand and sub-brands to support each other and add value to each other.

Aaker and Joachimsthaler (2000) defined brand architecture as an organizing structure of the brand portfolio that specifies brand roles and the nature of the relationship between brands, and argues that a coherent brand architecture can lead to impact, clarity, synergy, and leverage rather than market weak-ness, confusion, waste, and missed opportunities. Through brand management, CCA allows the main brand and sub-brands to leverage each other to better perpetuate CCA's corporate identity in the U.S. market.

4.1.2 Corporate Competence Building: Expand Business Scale and Increase Industry Visibility

Clear corporate identity is the first step in reputation creation, while good corporate competence is the fundamental guarantee for developing reputation. In the more than three decades since its entry into the U.S. market, CCA has experienced continued growth in business scale, substantial improvement in local industry rankings, and has won a number of industry awards – all of which are the most easily perceived reputation signals by stakeholders.

The Engineering News-Record (ENR), the world's most authoritative academic journal for engineering and construction, publishes an annual "International Contractor Ranking" based on corporate revenue, which reflects CCA's performance in the U.S. market: In 2010, CCA was ranked 286th on the "Top 400 Contractors in the U.S." list, and then gradually improved its ranking to remain among the top 50 in the country after 2015. It needs to be noted that very few of the top-ranked contractors in the U.S. are foreign-owned companies, and CCA is the only Chinese company on the list to date.

CCA's core competencies are global business experience, high level of construction quality and efficient management, which have been recognized by the industry in both China and the United States. Since 2002, CCA has received dozens of awards for outstanding projects from U.S. industry associations. In 2009, CCA won Luban Award, the highest award in China's construction industry, by the China Construction Industry Association for the Chancery Building of the Chinese Embassy in the U.S.; In 2013, CCA won Top 10 Bridges Award by the Roads & Bridges Magazine for the Alexander Hamilton Bridge project; In 2016 CCA won Diamond Award by American Council of Engineering Companies of New York for the MTA Fulton Center project.

The expansion of CCA's business enhances the brand's influence in the industry. In adding, it draws extensively on local suppliers and subcontractors and becomes part of the U.S. construction chain. Companies can only take social responsibility if they generate financial benefits (Doane & Abasta-Vilaplana, 2005), therefore the strong economic foundation is the pre-condition for CCA to carry out ethics activities.

4.1.3 Corporate Ethics Establishing: Conduct Volunteer Service as Team Building Activities

Considerable research reveals that employees' perceptions of corporate ethics affect their identification with the company (Kaptein and Van Dalen, 2000; Joyner and Payne, 2002; Brammer et al, 2007).

CCA always considers "giving back to the community" as an important corporate value, and encourages its employees to put this into practice. It actively organizes employees to participate in public welfare activities and combines team building with volunteer service, creating a stable tradition of employee volunteerism. Each year, a number of events are organized for employees at CCA, including the 9/11 Memorial Day Walk, JPMorgan Chase Corporate Challenge Run, Christmas Toy Drive, Food Pantry Drive and Volunteering at the NYC Marathon Supply Station. Moreover, the company sponsors the Liberty Science Center in Jersey City and regularly organizes employee participation in science, technology and math programs for local children. In addition to employees, CCA always encourages employees' family members to participate in these activities as well, so that they can all feel a sense of reward and become supporters of the corporate brand.

CCA hopes that by organizing their employees to participate in public service activities, they can build a successful team with a sense of social responsibility and a big picture. They believe that managing more than 3,500 employees well is the best way to promote the company's reputation.

Employee attitudes and behaviors will be affected by organizational culture and climate, and by whether CSR policies are couched in terms of compliance or in terms of value (Collier & Esteban, 2007). Social responsibility activities that are consistent with the organizational culture not only help to enhance employees' identification with the company, but also help to better recruit new employees and retain existing ones (Mirvis, 2012). By combining volunteer service with team building activities, CCA not only activates corporate social responsibility, but also allows employees to gain psychological satisfaction through participation.

4.2 CCA's Corporate Communication Strategies

As mentioned in the previous section, companies need to deliver their reputation signals to their stakeholders through communication strategies, which are the formal communication activities of the company.

The communications department is responsible for overseeing a wide range of communications activities. At present, CCA's overall corporate communication work is all handled by the Chairman's Office, with the Assistant to the Chairman's Office as the overall person in charge. Such a management structure makes CCA's communication strategies more oriented towards internal communication and industry communication.

4.2.1 Improve Employee Engagement by Internal Communication

As a multinational company with 98% of its employees are local hires, CCA need to improve communication, management and interaction of people from different cultures. In order to enhance employees' identification with the company, CCA launches a series of internal communication activities.

According to the cultural characteristics of American society, CCA proposes CCA Code of Conduct that articulates the basic standards and expectations that have long guided the company in work and daily decision-making (see Table 4.1). The principles set forth are clear and straightforward. They express CCA's core values and define its obligations, outlines the proper practices for the company, defines how they conduct business to benefit stakeholders.

Table 4.1 The CCA Code of Conduct

Dimension	Main Content
Honesty and Accountability	We are impeccable with our word and accountable with our behavior. Honesty and accountability are the cornerstones of our business.
Quality is Priority	Our brand is defined by the high-quality products and services we provide. We strive to achieve the best quality in every aspect of our professional and personal lives.
Professionalism and Dedication	Professionalism and dedication are fundamental to our success, as well as to the advancement of the industry. Our unique characteristics give us competitive advantages, and our professionalism earns us trust and credibility.
Adherence to Rules	Strict adherence to rules guarantees the stability and sustainability of an organization. By following rules and standards, an organization will operate and move forward on the right track.
Innovation is Key	Innovation brings vitality to an organization and enables it to adapt to the ever-changing world. We strive to create and maintain an environment that encourages innovation and embraces an entrepreneurial spirit.

Teamwork and Efficiency	Shared goals and working together define an outstanding team, which results in a highly efficient organization. We believe that consensus comes from communication and trust brings about synergy.
Collaboration and Cooperation	Collaboration and cooperation are core competencies for a successful organization, enabling it to operate with shared goals and common interests while reducing internal friction and creating values.
Honor and Broadmindedness	Honor is a principle and broadmindedness is an attitude. Both are key to building a successful organization. Honor and broadmindedness boost our internal fortitude and further our development.
Diligence and Tenacity	A true competitor is diligent and tenacious. Diligence and tenacity mean we persevere even in the face of adversity to overcome all obstacles.
Green Development	As a socially responsible company, we practice green development, demonstrating our commitment to preserving the environment. We not only care about the sustainability of our organization but that of the planet as well.

In order to make employees truly understand and practice the corporate philosophy, CCA has launched a series of communication activities within the company, such as training and meetings, to consolidate employee consensus.

For instance, as part of CCA's Chinese New Year tradition, the company organizes its annual compliance training session to kick off the New Year every year. The compliance training focuses on the importance of all employees working together to keep the CCA brand thriving and free from legal entanglements. Attendees usually be divided to teams to answer tricky questions on ethical situations they may encounter, which helps expand on what each employee has been taught for several years and reinforce their understanding of ethics and compliance. CCA believes that each employee is personally responsible and accountable for helping the company nourish a culture of honesty and integrity and maintain its reputation for the highest ethical standards.

Rituals, symbols and practices are important components of corporate culture. Through continuous internal communication, members of the company develop a "c collective programming of the mind" and recognize "the way we do things around here" (Hofstede et al, 1990). Individuals make sense of the world through the groups with which they identify. By projecting an attractive identity to employees, companies not only drive identification, but can steer the future direction of the company by effective socialization practices (Smidts et al, 2001)). For their part, employees that are inspired by the sense-giving initiatives of a company satisfy a psychological need for self-categorization ("I am a valuable person because I work for an important organization") and self-assessment ("I am valued for my work by the people within the organization").

4.2.2 Let Employees Deliver the Corporate Reputation Signals

A positive reputation works like a magnet which strengthens the attractiveness of an organization. From the research literature, we know that companies with a positive reputation can more easily attract and retain employees. The friendly working environment, excellent team management and a clear corporate vision can help build employees' confidence in the company's future; in turn, employees who have good perceptions of the company, such as admiration, trust and respect, are more willing to participate in internal corporate activities (Men,2012).

CCA knows that American culture is very individualistic, so they choose to take a very grassroots approach to developing corporate communication. Their media content is usually from the perspective of an ordinary person, rather than a grand narrative. For example, in order to better attract talents, CCA released a series of corporate promotional videos on social media, trying to let employees deliver the corporate reputation signals. Instead of introducing the company's achievements and development prospects from the corporate perspective, these promotional videos interviewed CCA's employees of various positions, colors and ages to share their work experiences, career gains, views on the company and understanding of the company's core values, so that each employee can become an endorser of the company's reputation. In the promotional videos, employees of CCA stated that they appreciate the family atmosphere, team spirit, innovation and space for career development at CCA, and feel protected in such an environment. Moreover, they believe that everyone is on the same point and going the same direction.

4.2.3 Professional Networking Priority over Social Networking

To make a message reach a specific target group on a satisfactory level for, the most effective channel should be used so that it could be performed in a relatively short time. For companies, each media channel has a different demographic and intended use. Twitter is a social networking channel for public communication, while LinkedIn is a professional networking channel for industry professionals, current employees and potential employees, and the usage of two channels by companies can show their different communication intentions (Kim et al, 2014). The book found that CCA's communication targets are more focused on employees and peer workers, while intentionally weakening the public-oriented communication, and such prioritization is reflected in its communication channel choice.

As of January 2022, CCA's official Twitter account @cca_cscec has posted 235 tweets and has only 415 followers while CCA's LinkedIn account has 20,528 followers. On LinkedIn, CCA maintains high frequency updates, mainly sharing internal corporate events, including holiday celebrations, team building activities and skills training programs, presenting the working atmosphere of the company.

It can be seen that CCA is more willing to use LinkedIn as a platform to present corporate culture and values than Twitter. By promoting internal activities and sharing employees' views, it can enhance the sense of belonging of employees, and help the company build a better employer image.

The reasons for doing so is that CCA's target audience is actually very fixed, they prefer to communicate with their colleagues, peers and potential employees on LinkedIn rather than with the public on Twitter, which indicated that their goal at this stage is to build a reputation in the industry.

4.3 The U.S. Media Coverage of CCA

After analyzing the primary and secondary communication of CCA, this section focuses on analyzing U.S. media coverage of CCA to examine the impact of the tertiary communication on CCA's reputation building.

In the Factiva news database, English-language news reports about CRRC in the five years ending September 1, 2020 were searched. After eliminating similar articles, a total of 1066 valid articles were obtained, and a 97,000 words corpus was build based on them.

The analyses were conducted using WORDij 3.0, a computer program (http:/wordij.net) that combines multiple analytic techniques including content analysis, computational linguistics, and network visualization. WORDij's WordLink program was used to identify concepts that co-occur with the word "China Construction America" in the corpus. The lower limit of word pair frequency was set to 3, that was, when the distance between two words was less than 3, the co-occurrence frequency between two words was calculated. A semantic network then was generated by linking these words based on the frequencies of their cooccurrences. Altogether 8526 nodes (words/terms/concepts) comprise the resultant network.

Next, the study loaded the network data, consisting of a list of concept node pairs and their aggregated frequencies, into Gephi0.9.2 to visualize the full network and the clusters. The sizes of the nodes are proportionate to the percentages of the nodes linked to them (See Figure 4.4).

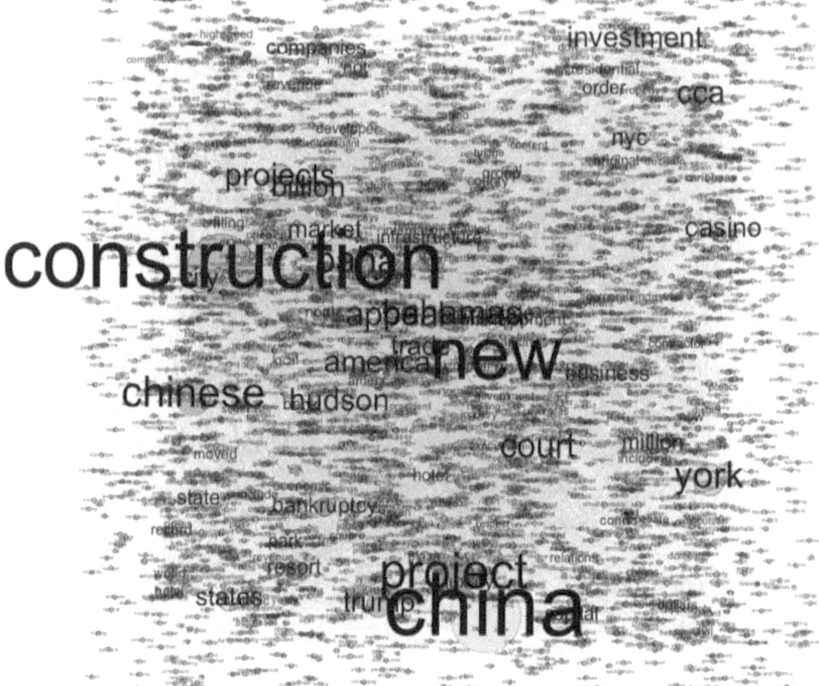

Figure 4.1 The Semantic Network of
"China Construction America"

4.3.1 Media Frames of CCA in the U.S.

Based on the semantic network above, the study used the
modularity algorithm created by Blondel et al. to segment the
semantic network structure (Blondel et al, 2008), and obtained a total
of 12 semantic clusters with a percentage of 1% or more, respectively:
11.65%, 8.24%, 7.52%, 7.09%, 4.49%, 3.6%, 2.83%, 2.23%, 1.72%,
1.17%, 1.14%, and 1%. Each cluster was composed of a series of high-
frequency word pairs, and they represented different dimensions of
the topic discussion. Five major clusters were selected for analysis in
this study and they are found to fall under three main media frames:
U.S.-China trade, project progress, and legal arbitration.

CCA is often found in news reports related to U.S.-China trade. High frequency words in this semantic cluster include Trump, investment, project, trade, dispute, and debt. The Trump administration added uncertainty to the global economic and political landscape, and the U.S. media launched a sustained focus on U.S.-China trade relations. Within the framework of this issue, the coverage focused on impact of the trade war on Chinese companies in the U.S. For example, in a story titled "U.S.-China trade war escalation leaves real estate in the dark," a spokesperson for CCA said that the imposition of tariffs on Chinese products has severely impacted contractors' imports of metals, tiles, and other building materials from China (Small and Sun, 2019).

Table 4.2 the Media Frame of U.S.-China Trade

Frame	U.S.-China Trade
High Frequency Words	construction, Chinese, Trump, billion, investment, engineering, trade, controversy, infrastructure, debt
Semantic Network of the Cluster	

Project progress is another typical frame for U.S. media coverage of CCA. Two semantic clusters fall under this frame, focusing on CCA's residential construction business and commercial construction business, respectively. The coverage is mainly focused on the progress of construction works. It should be noted that CCA has also participated in a number of U.S. infrastructure projects, yet they have received very little coverage in the U.S. For example, CCA completed the renovation of Alexander Hamilton Bridge as the contractor, and such a massive infrastructure project is rarely mentioned by U.S. media, while widely covered in China.

Table 4.3 the Media Frame of Project Progress

Frame	Project Progress	
Topic	Residential Construction Business	Commercial Construction Business
High Frequency Words	Hudson, luxury, park, development, residential, building	China, Miami, New York City, casino, hotel, expansion, economy
Semantic Network of the Cluster		

The third media frame for CCA is the legal arbitration frame, which focuses on CCA's Baha Mar resort project in Nassau, Bahamas, which is being sued over a legal dispute. High frequency words in the semantic cluster include Baha Mar, project, bankrupt, developer, bank, court, appeal, and so on.

Table 4.4 the Media Frame of Legal Arbitration

Frame	Legal Arbitration	
Topic	Baha Mar Resort Project	New York Court Arbitration
High Frequency Words	Baha Mar, Bahamas, engineering, bankruptcy, resort, developer, case, bank	New York, court, appeal
Semantic Network of the Cluster	bahamar bahamas million bankruptcy resort project	order city appeal new moved court york

The Baha Mar project is CSCEC's largest overseas investment, with a total investment of US$3.5 billion. The resort was scheduled to be completed in November 2014, but the project's majority shareholder, BML Properties, filed a lawsuit against CCA, charging it with "massive fraud and admitted sabotage", thus causing delays in the construction of the project. This series of lawsuits received extensive coverage in the U.S. media. From September 2014 to December 2017, the Wall Street Journal and the New York Times followed up with a total of 20 reports on this issue.

This study categorizes the news sources involved in the above 20 reports into six categories: CCA, BML Properties, Bahamian government, local Bahamian people, local employees of the project, and experts. The book found that the most prominent sources in the coverage were, in order, BML Properties (20), CCA (8), Bahamian government (8), local Bahamian people (4), experts (4) and local employees of the project (3).

Table 4.5 Information Sources Involved in the Wall Street Journal and the New York Times

Source	CCA	Properties	Bahamian Government	Local Bahamian People	Experts	Local Employees of the Project
Amount	8	20	8	4	4	3

In terms of the percentage of different sources, BML has a clear advantage, as it repeatedly expressed its opinion, accusing CCA of "massive fraud". The two media also interviewed a number of local Bahamian stakeholders, as victims of the delays, they tend to express their discontent with CCA, such as a local Bahamian employee interviewed by the Wall Street Journal who said that workers of CCA in the Bahamas are like "prisoners" who eat at the construction site, sleep in temporary shacks and never go to the beach. While these reports interviewed third-party experts and scholars, all of whom were from U.S. institutions or universities, were negative about Chinese companies' investments in the Americas.

In summary, the U.S. media coverage of CCA includes both discussions of U.S.-China trade and the progress of specific projects, but the largest proportion of it is the legal disputes and commercial controversies involved in CCA. In addition to using issue framing, the U.S. media further adjusted the weighting of sources to influence the direction of public opinion.

4.3.2 Media Image of CCA in the U.S.

It can be found that the media image of CCA in the U.S. is not very optimistic, mainly showing three negative characteristics, which obviously deviates from the corporate identity of CCA:

First, a company with Chinese government background. The U.S. media describes CCA as "Chinese government-owned," "state-run," "subsidiary of China State Construction Engineering Corporation," etc., which tends to make readers associate CCA with Chinese capital.

Second, a foreign competitor. In the report, the U.S. media analyzes the expansion of Chinese capital in the U.S. market and views the CCA as a foreign competitor that has risen rapidly after the financial crisis. At the same time, the U.S. media focuses more on the commercial projects undertaken by CCA and relatively less on the infrastructure projects in which CCA is involved. In fact, some of CCA's infrastructure projects have contributed to local communities, but are rarely mentioned in the coverage.

Third, a controversial engineering contractor. CCA's legal dispute over the Bahamas project is the focus of U.S. media attention. Although this dispute did not occur in the U.S. mainland, it attracted extensive attention due to its controversial and conflicting nature. It is evident that in an already unfavorable public opinion environment for Chinese companies, once negative news emerges, it is more likely to attract negative media coverage and further overshadow the company's efforts in other areas.

The bias of the U.S. media toward Chinese companies cannot be reversed by simple factual clarifications, but requires long-term media relations. However, this book finds that CCA tends to adopt a passive approach to U.S. media coverage, preferring to remain silent during controversies, which not only affects the efficiency of the company's response to public opinion but also exacerbates the bias in media coverage.

The reason for this is that CCA believes that they can't control what the U.S. media say about themselves, and what they can do is to operate in compliance so that the media can't find loopholes. They will never get involved in media wars.

In the controversy over the Baha Mar project, CCA appointed the defense attorneys as press spokesperson, and the company did not provide explanations or responses through any of its own communication channels. Such a response strategy makes CCA miss lots of opportunities to express itself.

A good relationship between company and media may not change the facts of the report, however, companies that are reachable and responsive can make journalists more willing to ask for their opinion when they conduct a news report. The book argues that CCA needs to readjust its media relations strategy and be more proactive in responding to the media in order to avoid exacerbating negative public opinion.

4.4 Summary

Reviewing the primary communication of CCA, the book finds that the company has a clear sense of the U.S. cognitive institutional environment and adapts it well by adjusting corporate identity. Based on its corporate identity, CCA carries out competence building and ethics establishing activities to accumulate reputation signals. However, when it comes to the secondary communication of CCA, we can see that CCA places more emphasis on internal communication than external communication. CCA improves employee engagement through internal communications, but does not devote efforts to maintaining public visibility, with holding a conservative and reactive approach to media coverage.

Such a communication strategy is the result of CCA's negative judgment of the public opinion environment in the U.S. The company believes that it is difficult to improve and reverse the public stereotype of Chinese SOEs, so it tries to "stay away" from U.S. media and avoid too much media exposure. In fact, such an attitude makes CCA miss many opportunities to express itself. The analysis of U.S. media coverage shows that there is a discrepancy between the media image and corporate identity of CCA, to bridge the gap requires more proactive external communication of the company.

Most SOEs do not take the initiative to communicate with the public as long as external public opinion does not affect the company's operation. As a result of this situation, the image of SOEs is often constructed by the media rather than shaped by themselves. Obviously, Chinese SOEs should improve their external public relations in order to effectively deal with potential reputational risks.

5. Reputation Building Strategy of China Railway Rolling Stock Corporation America

Just as successful companies need to be a supplier of choice, an employer of choice, and an investor of choice, they now have to become a neighbor of choice. They have to establish a reciprocal relationship and psychological contract with the community in order to be positioned positively in the community.

—— Burke, 1999

In September 2015, China Railway Rolling Stock Corporation (CRRC) established a manufacturing facility in Springfield, Massachusetts, where it undertakes a series of manufacturing projects and provides hundreds of local jobs. However, the market for rail transportation equipment in the U.S. is extremely competitive, and CRRC has encountered serious public controversy. From the perspective of overall corporate communication, this section analyzes CRRC's strategy for defending its reputation.

5.1 CRRC's Reputation Building Behaviors

5.1.1 Corporate Identity Positioning: A Company that Creates Value for Local Stakeholders

CRRC was created in June 2015 through a merger of two state-owned peers, CSR and CNR, with the goal of creating a synergy of "one plus one equals more than two." After the merger, CRRC repositioned its corporate identity and established the corporate mission of "connecting the world for the benefit of humanity".

CRRC stated that their mission is connecting the world through better mobility, and they strive to provide the most efficient solutions for sustainable development of railway transportation. Their vision embraces inclusion where collaboration is essential to enhance productivity, quality and innovation. To do this, they are shifting their overseas strategy from zouchuqu (go abroad) to rongjinqu (melt inside), in order for their overseas operations to co-exist and co-prosper with local economies.

The term "zouchuqu" refers to the long-running government policy of encouraging Chinese companies to expand their businesses beyond the country's borders, which embraces purchase of external assets and the conventional model of manufacturing low-cost products at home for export to overseas markets. "Rongjinqu," meanwhile, promotes the strategy of companies seeking to localize their overseas operations by integrating them with local economies where they have operations.

In an effort to court foreign railway operators that purchase CRRC's trains, the company aims at "local production of railway cars, local procurement of parts, employment of locals as plant workers and localization of management," working to build relationships with foreign customers and becoming a "good neighbor" in local communities. In other overseas markets, CRRC only need to deliver products and provide after-sales service, but in the U.S. market, they need to transfer technology, management and human resources to drive the local economy and provide the best value for Americans.

Granovetter (1985) argues that organizations can be embedded in specific social relationships through economic behavior. Based on embedding theory, scholars point out that localization of enterprises implies technological network embedding, business network embedding and relationship network embedding, which is the most sustainable way for companies to develop (Zhou et al., 2019). We can see that the identity positioning of CRRC is following the idea of localized embedding.

5.1.2 Corporate Competence Building: Develop Technology According to U.S. Standards

Since 2014, CRRC has received five orders in the U.S. totaling nearly $3 billion (see Table 5.1). According to data released by the American Public Transportation Association, there are around 500 transit agencies across the U.S., with an average annual purchase volume of around 1,000 vehicles, and CRRC has taken nearly 20% of the vehicle orders in this market in the past few years.

Table 5.1 Projects of CRRC America

Time	Project	Amount
October 2014	MBTA Orange & Red Line Metro Car Project	$567 million
April 2017	LACMTA HR4000 Heavy Rail Vehicle Project	$647 million
August 2017	SEPTA Multi-level Coach Project	$137.5 million

The rise of global markets and the development of technology have placed higher demands on companies to develop and utilize their resources. By focusing on innovative activities, companies can better respond to competitive pressures and create revenue streams (Huse et al, 2005), and the business success of CRRC stems from the company's emphasis on product development and technological innovation.

According to the regulations, all railroad vehicles entering the U.S. market must pass the identification tests. Therefore, CRRC's products and machinery parts need to be certified before being placed on the U.S. market. They had to go through various tests to meet the criteria, and it took them 39 months to get qualified to bid for the New York subway.

CRRC also improves its market competitiveness through patent develop. According to the public data, CRRC currently ranks first in the world for the number of valid patents in the field of rail transportation, and owns many U.S. patents. In addition to meeting product standards, China Railway Corporation also improves its market competitiveness through patent inventions. According to public data, CRRC currently ranks first in the world for the number of patents in the rail transportation field, and has a number of U.S. patents. The U.S. is one of the strictest countries in the world in terms of patent examination. The successful approvals of patent reflect CRRC's technical level and are also conducive to CRRC's further development in the U.S. market.

Furthermore, CRRC has set up research centers jointly with the University of Southampton, the University of Birmingham, TU Dresden, Ruhr University Bochum and Czech Technical University in Europe, as well as the University of Illinois, the University of Michigan and Virginia Polytechnic Institute and State University in the U.S., which provide platforms for academic and technical exchanges.

Studies show that for high-tech enterprises in China, increasing research and development investment is an important way to achieve international competitiveness of companies (Zhu & Yang, 2019), and CRRC's corporate competence development route fits this argument. By developing patents and establishing research centers, CRRC provides impetus for corporate innovation and accumulates reputation signals about corporate competence.

5.1.3 Corporate Ethics Establishing: Embed in Industry Chains and Integrate into Local Communities

For CRRC, insisting on localization is not only a subjective choice of corporate identity positioning, but also an objective requirement of the U.S. business environment. The U.S. has strict regulations for the railroad equipment manufacturing industry, which means CRRC has to comply with complex legal requirements and fulfill more social responsibilities during project execution.

5.1.3.1 Building Local Partnerships

For multinational companies, corporate compliance with local laws and regulations is the cornerstone of sustainable business development (Parker & Nielsen, 2009). CRRC's main business is to provide railroad equipment to the U.S. government, which has strict requirements for public funding expenditures and project approvals.

In 1978, the U.S. Congress began placing domestic content restrictions on federally funded transportation projects that are carried out by nonfederal government agencies such as state and local governments. These restrictions, which have changed over the years, are commonly referred to as the Buy America Act, or more simply, Buy America.

Buy America refers to several similar statutes and regulations that apply when federal funds are used to support projects involving highways, public transportation, aviation, and intercity passenger rail. Unless a nationwide or project-specific waiver is granted, Buy America requires the use of U.S.-made iron and steel and the domestic production and assembly of other manufactured goods, particularly the production of rolling stock (railcars and buses) used in federally funded public transportation and Amtrak's intercity passenger rail service. A separate law requires that at least half the value of products imported by sea for federally supported transportation projects be transported in U.S.-flag ships.

In addition to this, the U.S. Department of Transportation requires that any company that has a contract with the Department of Transportation needs to subcontract a certain percentage of its business to MBE (Minority Business Enterprise), WBE (Woman Business Enterprise) and/or DBE (Disadvantaged Business Enterprise).

Consequently, CRRC is required to source at least 65% of the materials for the production process locally in the U.S., and to hire local workers for vehicle assembly. Moreover, CRRC needs to include and utilize minority (MBE), women (WBE) and disadvantaged businesses enterprises (DBE) into their procurement processes.

The above regulations obviously compress the profit margin of CRRC and affect the operational efficiency and management costs of the company. However, the mandatory localization measures also prompt CRRC to develop local partnerships and better integrate into the local business environment. To meet the requirements of the Buy America Act, CRRC needs to develop a local supplier chain, both with large rail companies and with small and medium-sized companies. At the same time, in order to hire skilled U.S. workers, CRRC has to work hard to gain the support of local labor organizations and establish good labor relations. These efforts are in line with the compliance requirements of the U.S. market and provide opportunities for CRRC to assume local social responsibility. CRRC stated that they value every employee and partner, strengthen long-term cooperation with local industry chain partners, listen to the voice of customers, and join forces with stakeholders to create value and achieve long-term sustainable development.

5.1.3.2 Become a Member of the Local Community

Ismail (2009) viewed community as a group of people sharing a common purpose, who are interdependent for the fulfillment of certain needs, who live in close proximity and interact on a regular basis. There are shared expectations for all members of the group and responsibility taken from those expectations. The group is respectful and considerate of the individuality of other persons within the community. In a community there is a sense of community which is defined as the feelings of cooperation, of commitment to the group welfare, of willingness to communicate openly, and of responsibility to and for others as well as to one' s self.

In addition to conducting the production and delivery of products, CRRC is also actively building relationships with the Springfield community. When it first entered the U.S., CRRC intended to build a factory in Springfield. In the planned factory area, there was a 100-year-old red brick house that originally belonged to the Westinghouse Electric Company which held the memories of the local industrial civilization. In the process of building the factory, CRRC staff noticed that the local residents did not want the house to be demolished, so after internal discussion and evaluation, CRRC decided to invest more in preserving the old house and refurbish it for office use, which earned favors from the local people. On the groundbreaking day of the factory, local residents came up with a slogan "Welcomes CRRC".

Figure 5.1 the Refurbished Red Brick
House (Photo by the Author)

It is worth pointing out that Springfield was an important heavy manufacturing base of the eastern United States in the 1930s and 1940s, however, after the end of World War II, Springfield's manufacturing industry gradually declined. Restarting the manufacturing industry has always been the desire of the local labor unions, so when CRRC moved into Springfield, they came forward to the company to seek cooperation. With the assistance of the local union, CRRC successfully recruited the first batch of mechanical and electrical workers and subsequently provided more than 200 jobs to the community.

CRRC also established partnerships with local colleges and Springfield's Regional Employment Council to promote recruitment. These partnerships not only help CRRC develop its own human resources, but also boost the manpower needs of downstream suppliers. Even a specialized Chinese language teaching institution has emerged in Springfield to help residents obtain better job development opportunities.

CRRC's arrival in Springfield has restarted the manufacturing industry here, not only creating local jobs but also boosting the economy, which is certainly a good thing for the local government and residents. In many cases, they don't look at the problem from the perspective of a factory, but from the perspective of a community member. For example, after the first subway cars were produced, CRRC planned to build a rail transportation line to deliver the product to Boston, but the railroad would run through a neighbor's property. It was CRRC's well-maintained community relations that made the neighbor to approve the construction of the line, enabling more economical and convenient transportation of the product.

In the process of production and operation, CRRC has achieved to embed its technology network, business network and relationship network in the local community and become an important member of it.

5.2 The U.S. Media Coverage of CRRC

Despite a series of localization efforts, CRRC faces an uncertain public opinion environment, characterized by polarized local and national public opinion, which poses important challenges to its reputation building. In order to better understand the external interference factors in CRRC's reputation building, this section analyzes relevant media coverage in the U.S.

A macro-meso-micro research approach is adopted in this section, which first analyzing the semantic network of related reports, then examining which media frames different semantic clusters fall into, and finally conducting a textual analysis of representative news reports.

5.2.1 Media Frames of CRRC in the U.S.

In the Factiva news database, English-language news reports about CRRC in the five years ending September 1, 2020 were searched. After eliminating similar articles, a total of 1066 valid articles were obtained, mainly from national media such as the Wall Street Journal and the New York Times, as well as regional media in Massachusetts.

A corpus of 230,000 words was built based on the articles. WORDij's WordLink program was used to identify concepts that co-occur with the word "CRRC MA" and "China Railway Rolling Stock Corp Massachusetts" in the corpus. The lower limit of word pair frequency was set to 3, that was, when the distance between two words was less than 3, the co-occurrence frequency between two words was calculated. A semantic network then was generated by linking these words based on the frequencies of their cooccurrences. Altogether 20237 nodes (words/terms/concepts) comprise the resultant network.

Next, the study loaded the network data, consisting of a list of concept node pairs and their aggregated frequencies, into Gephi0.9.2 to visualize the full network and the clusters. The sizes of the nodes are proportionate to the percentages of the nodes linked to them (See Figure 5.2).

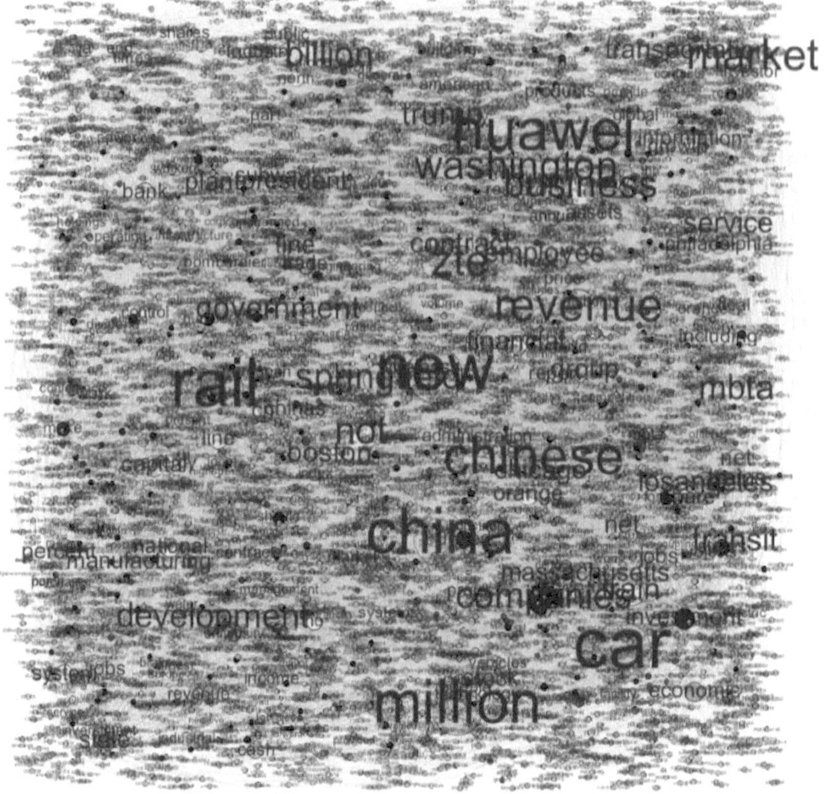

Figure 5.2 The Semantic Network of "China
Railway Rolling Stock Corp Massachusetts"

Based on the semantic network above, the study used the modularity algorithm to segment the semantic network structure and obtained a total of 14 semantic clusters with a percentage of 1% or more. Five major clusters were selected for analysis in this study and they are found to fall under three main media frames: trade conflicts, economic impact and project progress.

The trade conflict is the most notable media frame, and two semantic clusters fall under this frame, focusing on cybersecurity controversy and the U.S. government initiatives, respectively.

Since 2018, trade conflicts between the U.S. and China have escalated, with the U.S. sanctioning Chinese telecommunications companies such as Huawei and blacklisting 70 companies for trade controls. During the same period, CRRC prepared to bid on the Washington Metro project, but some lobby groups and Senate members claimed that the subway cars produced by CRRC could track the movements of members of Congress and intelligence officials, and steal user data if WIFI is installed. These speculations have received considerable coverage by the U.S. media, with "Huawei," "car," and "wireless" being the main high-frequency words.

In addition, the Trump administration's initiatives toward China also appeared in related reports, in August 2018, the U.S. House and Senate issued a decision to ban the use of federal funds to purchase rolling stock from China, which sparked a media discussion about whether U.S. subways should become international trade bargaining chips, with "Trump," "trade," "development," and "tariffs" appearing frequently in related reports.

Table 5.2 the Media Frame of Trade Conflicts

Frame	Trade Conflicts	
Topic	Cybersecurity Controversy	the U.S. Government Initiatives
High Frequency Words	China, railroad, Huawei, carriage wireless, network, manufacturer	Trump, administration, trade, economy, development, tariffs
Semantic Network of the Cluster	huawei plant zte government rail springfield chinese china manufacturing net car	trump president trade administration development economic investment

The economic impact caused by CRRC's operations in the U.S. is another important frame for U.S. media coverage of CRRC, including industry impact and regional impact as two topics.

On the one hand, the U.S. media has always been wary of the rapid growth of Chinese companies in the U.S. market. In a report, the Chicago Tribune said, "China's model of state-led capitalism has contributed to the loss of U.S. jobs and the hollowing out of industrial base as dumped and subsidized imports surged into our market since China joined the WTO in 2001." Some media believe that CRRC, as a Chinese state-owned enterprise with government background, cannot compete fairly in the market. The Wall Street Journal, for example, noted in a report that "The SOEs are also supported by policies, including, but not limited to, discriminatory loan rates, tax rates, direct subsidies, protected home markets, lax labor and environmental regulation, and exchange rate misalignment."

On the other hand, some local Massachusetts media places more emphasis on the impact of CRRC on regional economic development, with "revenue," "employee," and "jobs" are high frequency words. Business West, a local media in Springfield, where CRRC's Massachusetts factory is located, has repeatedly mentioned the role of CRRC in boosting the regional economy and increasing employment.

Table 5.3 the Media Frame of Economic Impact

Frame	Economic Impact	
Topic	Industry Impact	Regional Impact
High Frequency Words	new, contract, Washington, Chicago. Massachusetts, Philadelphia, traffic, transportation, metro	revenue, service, employee, jobs, investments, growth, assets
Semantic Network of the Cluster		

While most of the U.S. media focused on the economic impact of CRRC and the security controversy it caused, some media also kept an eye on CRRC's rolling stock production and delivery.

CRRC's first order in the U.S. market is for the manufacture of Boston Orange Line subway cars, which is expected to be completed in 2023. The overall progress of the project, from contract award to product delivery, are continuous reported in local media. High frequency words in this media frame include "Boston," "built," and "Massachusetts Department of Transportation (MBTA)".

Table 5.4 the Media Frame of Project Progress

Frame	Project Progress
High Frequency Words	Boston, Orange Line, built, MBTA
Semantic Network of the Cluster	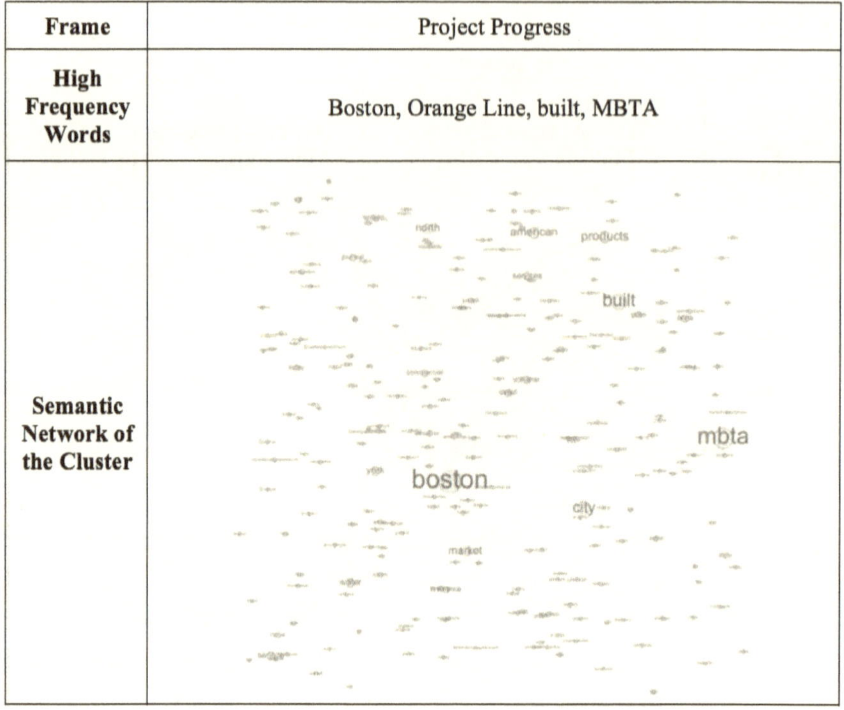

5.2.2 Media Image of CRRC in the U.S.

To further explore the characteristics of U.S. media coverage, this section compares the differences in coverage of CRRC between regional and national media.

In the Factiva news database, the regional media with most reports on CRRC is Business West, and the national media is the Wall Street Journal, with 26 and 17 articles respectively. Founded in 1984 and headquartered in Springfield, Massachusetts, Business West began as a semi-monthly financial magazine in western Massachusetts and later became a regional business news website. Headquartered in New York, The Wall Street Journal is one of the most widely circulated and influential newspapers in the United States, focusing on business and political coverage.

After reading through all the articles, this section uses the method of discourse analysis to interpret them. The analysis of discourse is, necessarily, the analysis of language in use. As such, it cannot be restricted to the description of linguistic forms independent of the purposes or functions which these forms are designed to serve in human affairs (Brown & Yule, 1983). The approach of discourse analysis also helps to reveal the hidden power and ideology behind the language.

Fairclough (1989, 1992) proposes that the critical discourse analysis of a text should pass through the three stages of description, interpretation of the relationship between text and interaction, and explanation of the relationship between interaction and social context. With this in mind, this section first analyzes the themes of the articles, and then examines them at the description, interpretation, and explanation dimension, respectively.

5.2.2.1 Discourse Analysis of Business West's Coverage

Business West focuses on Springfield's economic development and the role CRRC plays in it, with articles centered on the following themes (see Table5.5).

In September 2015, CRRC officially laid the groundwork in Springfield, bringing continued economic dividends to the community. Business West has consistently reported on the positive impact CRRC has had on local employment growth, supply chain development, and optimization of community relations. Meanwhile, Business West also looks at Springfield's economic development policies, noting that CRRC is an important economic driver in the ten-year blueprint released by the local Economic Development Planning Committee. As for the negative issues involved in CRRC, such as the controversy of cybersecurity, Business West did not mention it at all.

Table 5.5 Themes of Business West's Coverage

Theme	Amount
Economic Revival of Springfield	14
Economic Development Policy of Springfield	6
Operations of CRRC	6
Total	26

Business West uses verbs such as "welcoming," "expect," and "look forward" for the arrival of CRRC, and uses "confidence builder," "evidence of renaissance," "signs of progress" and "a good amount of luck" to describe the impact of CRRC on the local economy. This shows that all stakeholders in Springfield have high expectations for the CRRC and are satisfied with its development. In terms of the use of attribute for CRRC, Business West primarily highlights CRRC's professional status and economic strength. Although in some cases Business West mentions that CRRC is backed by Chinese capital, it does not emphasize CRRC's government background (see Table 5.6).

Table 5.6 Business West's Use of Attribute for CRRC

A subsidiary of the China-based world leader in rail-car manufacturing
Large employer
Springfield's brand
Chinese rail-car manufacturing giant
Important regional economic-development projects
Chinese-owned Rail Corp
Chinese rail-car manufacturer
Subway-car manufacturing plant
Chinese rail car maker
Rail car builder

A count of all 26 Business West articles on CRRC reveals the following distribution of news sources. As shown in the table below, the most frequent news sources in the coverage were, in order, companies in Springfield (26), Springfield Government (19), NGOs in Springfield (7), public (5), experts (5) and others (3). On the whole, Business West's news sources are made up of local economic, political, and academic figures, who mainly analyze the economic situation, discuss economic policies, and state the impact of CRRC on local economic development.

Table 5.7 Information Sources Involved in the Business West

Source	Public	Springfield Government	Companies in Springfield	NGOs in Springfield	Experts	Others
Amount	5	19	26	7	5	3

5.2.2.2 Discourse Analysis of the Wall Street Journal's Coverage

As a national business newspaper, the Wall Street Journal's reports on CRRC covered more political and economic issues, and the themes of coverage were negative in almost all cases. As the following table shows, the Wall Street Journal highlights the information security controversy that CRRC involves and the threat CRRC poses to the U.S. rail equipment manufacturing industry. For example, in a report, the Wall Street Journal noted that CRRC had won the order with a bid that was 15 percent lower than that of its competitors, posing a threat to the global rail equipment manufacturing industry. In addition, the Wall Street Journal also noticed the economic situation in Springfield, but unlike Business West's optimism, the WSJ said the city's economy remains fragile despite the presence of companies such as CRRC in Springfield.

Table 5.8 Themes of Wall Street Journal's Coverage

Theme	Amount
Information Security Controversy Over CRRC Produced Subway Cars	8
CRRC Threatens Rail Equipment Manufacturing Industry	6
Current Economic Situation in Springfield	2
US Company Terminates High-speed Rail Deal with China	1
Total	17

In the information security controversy over CRRC, the Wall Street Journal described the blockage of the CRRC project in Congress as "Irritating lawmakers," "derail" and "banned," highlighting the seriousness of the incident.

The Wall Street Journal called CRRC's participation in the bidding "undersell" and said the U.S. rail industry would "fades away" under CRRC's influence, and used the phrase "licking its wounds" to describe the impact on CRRC's competitors. It also described CRRC's market expansion as "scooped up", "make deep inroads" and "gain a bigger foothold", giving CRRC's global market expansion an aggressive tone.

As for the Wall Street Journal's use of attribute for CRRC, as seen in the table below, it highlights CRRC's SOE background and emphasizes CRRC's financial advantages in its coverage, which tends to make readers link Chinese government capital to CRRC's market development.

Table 5.9 Wall Street Journal's Use of Attribute for CRRC

The state-owned titan which has built plants in Chicago and Springfield
Dominate investment-grade bond issuance in China and often enjoy cheaper bank loans as well
U.S. subsidiaries of China's state-owned CRRC Corp.
A state-owned entity, enjoys a host of advantages over private firms
Chinese rail giant

Chinese government-owned
Ranks as the world's largest train maker with more than $30 billions of sales
A company in China's government-run train industry
A giant rail-equipment manufacturer
Supplies a majority of China's railcars and also manufactures bullet trains

A count of the Wall Street Journal's news sources shows that its most prominent sources are the U.S. Congress, including two members of the Transportation and Infrastructure Committee, seven legislators opposing CRRC, and one Massachusetts legislator who supports CRRC. The second major sources were CRRC's competitors, including Siemens of Germany, Alstom of France, and Bombardier of Canada, who were interviewed by the newspaper about the challenges posed to them by the CRRC's development. The views of members from the Rail Security Alliance, a lobbying group formed specifically to oppose CRRC's market expansion, have also appeared several times in the reports of Wall Street Journal, where they have emphasized to the media the urgency of investigating the information security of CRRC produced subway cars. Responses from CRRC's spokesperson and chief legal counsel appeared five times in the coverage to provide clarification on the controversy involving CRRC. The White House administration served as a source four times to show the administration's concern for national security. There were also U.S. industry experts, economic experts and university academics who spoke out on rail manufacturing and the U.S.-China trade relationship.

It is clear from the above analysis that the Wall Street Journal's news sources are not balanced enough, with stakeholder groups opposed to CRRC given more opportunities to speak out.

Table 5.10 Information Sources Involved in the Wall Street Journal

Source	U.S. Congress	Competitors of CRRC	Rail Security Alliance	CRRC	The White House	Experts	Others
Total	9	8	5	5	4	3	5

5.2.2.3 Divided Media Images and the Political and Economic Motivations Behind Them

Fairclough always emphasizes the dialectical relationship between language and society, arguing that, on the one hand, social structures influence discursive practices, and on the other hand, discourse is constantly constructing social structures (Wang, & Yang, 2008). For news coverage, differences in the standpoints of different media are reflected in different news discourses, which in turn have an impact on public perception.

Reviewing the image construction of CRRC by the two media, it can be found that: In the coverage of Business West, CRRC is a major foreign investment force that has energized the local economy and is a testament to Springfield's economic renaissance. In the Wall Street Journal, however, CRRC is the controversial Chinese railroad equipment manufacturing giant that has impacted the U.S. market.

There are two main reasons for this discrepancy. On the one hand, the differences between the two media in terms of coverage themes are influenced by news value criteria. "Close to home" is an important value criterion among the 8 typical news values in Western countries (Zheng & Liu, 2010). As a local newspaper in Springfield, Business West's audience is local residents, so it focuses more on topics close to home, such as factory construction, job opportunities, and community development. Whereas for the Wall Street Journal, as an international daily newspaper based in New York City, it is more concerned with global economic issues. On the other hand, the difference in reporting tendencies is importantly related to the positions of the media themselves. Business West is a beneficiary of Springfield's economic development, so the news coverage will positively recognize CRRC's regional contributions, and the tone of the coverage will be more in line with the audience's psychological expectations of an economic upturn. The Wall Street Journal, on the other hand, upholds a typically American conservative position and is highly influential in establishment conservative circles. Some scholars have pointed out that although the American media has always boasted objectivity, truthfulness, and impartiality, it essentially serves power and capital (Li & Chang, 2012). Since 2018, the U.S. government has continued to crack down on Chinese companies in its policies, and the Wall Street Journal has been a supporter of U.S. foreign policy. It places China's role in opposition to the U.S. government, U.S. companies and even global companies, with a clear China threat rhetoric in its reports.

Overall, while the CRRC has received support from the local media, it is clear that the national media has more influence on public opinion. Viewing CRRC as an economic threat by the national media has had a repressive effect on CRRC's national reputation. Faced with such a severe public opinion environment, CRRC needs to respond urgently.

5.3 CRRC's Corporate Communication Strategies

Compared with other companies, CRRC's communication strategies were more unique: soon after entering the U.S. market, CRRC experienced the continuous deterioration of Sino-U.S. relations and a boycott by its competitors, so its communication objectives, resources and channels were almost entirely focused on responding to the corporate crisis.

In August 2018, some Senators proposed to ban the U.S. government from purchasing railroad locomotives produced by foreign state-owned enterprises, and this proposal was clearly aimed at CRRC, directly putting the company at risk of exiting the U.S. market. Faced with the reputation dilemma, CRRC clarified its communication strategy centered on crisis response, hired the former spokesperson of the Boston Transportation Authority as the head of corporate public relations, and finally won operating space under the severe public opinion situation.

5.3.1 Conduct Lobbying Activities to Improve Government Relations

Lobbying is every activity carried out with the objective of directly or indirectly influencing the formulation or implementation of the policy and decision-making process regarding legislative or regulatory activities (Zhao, 2005). The U.S. Constitution provides that, international companies can obtain lobbying services to influence legislation in the U.S., and to work toward favorable regulations.

CRRC has partner lobbying firms in cities such as Boston, Los Angeles, New York and Chicago to communicate with local governments in a legal manner. It can be found in the database of the U.S. lobbying information website that CRRC paid $80,000 and $120,000 for political lobbying in 2018 and 2019, respectively. Faced with pressure from Congress to ban the business, CRRC first set up a crisis response team with the spokesperson as the core, responded to media inquiries immediately, and hired a Washington-based government lobbying expert to negotiate with members of Congress. The head of public relations at CRRC was in very frequent contact with their lobbying team in Washington, they discuss issues remotely and fight for a common goal together.

In its communications with the government, CRRC highlighted three main points:

First, for the most prominent cybersecurity controversy, CRRC stressed that all of the company's technology control systems meet the standards of the Buy America Act, and that all product parts come from U.S. suppliers and are installed by American workers.

Second, in response to the accusation that CRRC underbid for contracts, the company provided the government with a report, pointing out that the government's decision to select a high-quality, reasonably priced product was the most responsible decision for taxpayers, and emphasizing that each CRRC bid was a win-win choice for both the company and the government.

Third, regarding concerns about CRRC's excessive involvement in U.S. infrastructure development, the lobbying team demonstrated the regional economic impact of CRRC's entry into the United States. Lobbyists provided hiring data of CRRC to the Congress, and stated that CRRC offers competitive wages to local workers and is working to improve their quality of life and occupational skills. In addition, they collected endorsement letters from unions, suppliers and cooperative customers which described the contribution of CRRC to the local market.

5.3.2 Developing Communication Channels for Public Opinion Counterattack

One of CRRC's main opponents is the Rail Safety Coalition (RSA). RSA is a coalition of North American rail car manufacturers, rail component suppliers, unions, and steel interests that are formed in response to the merging of China's state-owned rail manufacturers. The coalition has a long history of issuing statements against CRRC and engaging in lobbying of lawmakers. On its official website, RSA has collected the views of various people against CRRC, and also launched an online petition campaign to oppose the U.S. the U.S. government's procurement of CRRC products in the name of national security.

In order to clarify the facts clearly and efficiently, CRRC set up a dedicated fact check website. The website includes multiple sections such as corporate announcements, employment data, legal documents, testimonials, and media news.

The announcement on the front page of the website clearly indicates that all parts of CRRC products are not produced by Chinese companies. To prove this, CRRC has published a diagram of the company's supply chain and a map of supplier distribution to demonstrate that the company strictly follows U.S. law in its supply chain selection and that no part of the chain offers the possibility of espionage.

In addition, the website releases a fact sheet on the cybersecurity controversy, listing four facts below.

Fact 1: Transit rail car vehicles purchased from China pose no threat to the United States. As there are no US owned rail car manufacturers, US transit agencies must procure their public transit vehicles from international manufacturers. Similar to other companies in the industry, CRRC abides by the same standards and processes and works under the same supervisory review required by transit agencies. CRRC adheres to the rigorous cybersecurity practices outlined within a cybersecurity analysis based on a U.S. Department of Defense military system safety standard. The agency and third-party consultants review the entire process through design, software development, manufacturing of products and small parts testing, safety certification, reliability verification, and other crucial area.

Fact 2: The passenger rail car industry is one of the biggest expenses to government and taxpayers. Entering a new market involves strategic expansion. CRRC focuses on providing a modern efficient vehicle at the most economical price using the best and most qualified suppliers. CRRC's bid on its first U.S. contract was determined to be reasonable, responsible, and balanced. CRRC has advantages in localization. Through decades of world-wide experience, CRRC's production model providing for the manufacturing of vehicles in the United States has proven cost efficient and successful. CRRC pricing is in line with the bidding/awarding pricing of the recent 10 years procurement in the United States.

Fact 3: All rail car builders use similar supply chain for major systems. CRRC partners with reputable, qualified USA system suppliers on Propulsion/Traction Control System, Auxiliary Power System, Vehicle Monitoring System, HVAC. There is no difference between CRRC's US supply chain and other competing companies'.

Fact 4: CRRC is committed to transparency and is eager to partner with the transit industry to ensure cybersecurity protocol is standardized and adhered to. CRRC calls for a transit industry discussion to enhance cybersecurity standards, including management systems.

CRRC has also been strengthening its media relations, responding to media inquiries in a timely manner and providing them with illustrated and logical fact sheets in an effort to dispel media bias. Furthermore, CRRC has invited influential media to the factory for on-site interviews, for example, the Consumer News and Business Channel (CNBC) conducted a live broadcast at the factory, interviewing managers and employees for their perspectives.

In its business operations, CRRC has always made localization a priority. Once Congress passes the ban on CRRC, it will not only mean that CRRC will withdraw from the U.S. market, but also mean that hundreds of people will lose their jobs and cause damage to the local economy. In such cases, CRRC launches grassroots advocacy to mobilize stakeholders of Springfield community. Doorley and Garcia (2011) have pointed out that grassroots advocacy is an indirect lobbying activity that can influence legislators' attitudes when the content of the defense is sufficiently persuasive.

Specifically, CRRC produced a series of short videos that interviewed stakeholders such as the company's suppliers, local union leaders and factory workers about their views on CRRC. These short videos show CRRC's positive role in promoting employment, contributing to the community, and driving the development of the industry chain from different perspectives, which echoes the company's business philosophy of "localization development". In the short videos, stakeholders stated their viewpoints about CRRC (see table 5.11).

Table 5.11 Stakeholders' Viewpoints about CRRC in Short Videos

Stakeholder	Response Highlights	Viewpoints
Supply Chain Management Company	Policy Legitimacy	For the MBTA project, there is a 65% requirement to Buy America and CCRC fulfills that need.
Local Business Agent	Local Contributions	CRRC is offering Springfield residents blue-collar jobs, and offering them great benefit package. They're putting Springfield residents to work.

Regional Employment Board	Local Contributions	Job creation and economic development is a critical part for Springfield to get accomplished. CRRC is putting people to work and growing the region economy.
Fire Equipment Company	Industry Contributions	CRRC has helped women-owned business grow. Its orders account for approximately 40 percent of our annual revenue.
Union Production Worker	Employee Comments	The diversity of CRRC brings different backgrounds, different ideas, different thoughts that's very useful to this industry.

The above analysis shows that in the face of the controversy, CRRC chose a proactive crisis response approach, mobilizing stakeholders from multiple fields and clarifying facts in various ways.

Finally, in December 2019, thanks to CRRC's efforts, the U.S. government did not pass the ban on CRRC directly, but instead gave CRRC a two-year grace period during which CRRC can bid for any transit contract other than with WAMATA (Washington DC transits system). And if CRRC can get more orders within two years, there is a reason to convince lawmakers to extend the investment permit for CRRC afterwards, bringing more opportunities for local manufacturing.

5.4 Summary

Reviewing the case of CRRC, it can be found that the regulative and normative institutional environment is the primary consideration in its process of reputation building. Under the U.S. government's mandatory localization requirements, CRRC fulfills laws and regulations while meeting the moral expectations of the local community.

In the primary communication, CRRC has taken the responsibility of driving local economic development, and accumulated a good community reputation, which can be seen from the local media reports. However, CRRC is facing the crisis of withdrawing from the U.S. market due to competitor attacks and changes in U.S.-China relations, and the American national media has been reporting negatively about CRRC, which means that the tertiary communication of the company is not very favorable. In response to a severe corporate crisis, CRRC has developed secondary communication activities aimed at crisis response. CRRC hired local PR experts to handle government lobbying and media communications, while actively inviting stakeholders to endorse for the company. Eventually, CRRC influenced the government resolution, allowing the company to continue operating in the U.S. market.

The CRRC case shows us that while sometimes the macro institutional environment sets up obstacles to business development, the accumulation of local reputation capital and proactive communications can help the company in addressing reputation challenges.

6. The Model of Overseas Reputation Building for Chinese SOEs

6.1 Internal and External Challenges to the Reputation Building of Chinese SOEs

Through the research of the two cases, the book finds that two SOEs had different reputation building strategies and developed different reputation effects according to the differences in internal communication objectives and external opinion situation. Although the practices of both companies have their own highlights and merits, overall, Chinese SOEs still confront many problems and challenges in the process of building reputation in the U.S.

6.1.1 External Challenges: American Institutional Power Influences Media Coverage

On the one hand, studies have shown that, regardless of partisan leanings, the U.S. media's fundamental position in foreign affairs coverage is to defend the country's interests (Lang, 2003; Cui, 2017). In particular, as the U.S. government continues to introduce containment policies against China, arguments such as "China's rise" and "China threat" frequently appear in media reports (Wu Fei,

2015). On the other hand, the U.S. media system is typically a liberal model, with the vast majority of U.S. media being commercial, which are essentially corporate properties that struggle to attract consumers in order to survive (Curran et al, 2009). With this logic, U.S. media will try to provide coverage that meets the psychological expectations of their audience to achieve profitability.

By analyzing the media framing and discursive strategies of U.S. media coverage on Chinese SOEs, it can be found that: political framework is prevalent in U.S. media coverage, and the media tend to link the development of Chinese enterprises to China's national strategy, using political discourse to explain the business behavior of Chinese SOEs. The U.S. media generally emphasizes the government background, state subsidies and industry monopoly status of Chinese SOEs, and characterizes the development of Chinese SOEs' business in the U.S. as aggression. In addition, reports on Chinese SOEs focus mainly on controversial issues they involved, while generally ignoring their contributions to the livelihoods of local communities.

In particular, it should be noted that in recent years, the U.S. government has repeatedly suppressed the normal operations of Chinese companies on the grounds of national security. In the case of this book, CRRC has encountered a typical national security controversy, which directly affects the legitimacy of CRRC's operation. In the 1990s, the Copenhagen School proposed the Securitization Theory. The main argument of securitization theory is that in international relations an issue becomes a security issue not because something constitutes an objective threat to the state (or another referent object), but rather because an actor has defined something as existential threat to some object's survival (Buzan et al, 1998). As can be seen, the U.S. government and the U.S. media together form an action group that constantly interprets Chinese companies as a security threat

In short, under the combined influence of institutional power and media coverage, the U.S. public has gradually developed a bias against Chinese SOEs, which poses additional challenges to the construction of Chinese SOEs' reputation in the United States.

6.1.2 Internal Challenge: Chinese SOEs Lack Subjective Drivers for Reputation Building

In the tough public opinion environment, the willingness of Chinese SOEs to build their reputation is not yet clear. In the interviews, SOE leaders mentioned the word "branding" more often, but rarely used "reputation" to refer to the direction of corporate development.

In fact, corporate branding and corporate reputation, although closely linked, are not exactly equivalent. Branding is a marketing concept for which the main targets are customers and consumers (Hatch and Schultz, 2008; Hatch and Schultz, 2001), while reputation is the overall perception of the company by various stakeholders, we can say that brand building is a stage of reputation building.

In terms of communication objectives, the book finds that the main objectives of Chinese SOEs are to improve sales performance, maintain customer relationships, gain government support, and reach internal consensus, etc. Their communication targets are primarily customers, government, and employees, but rarely consider delivering reputation signals to publics. This is due to the fact that SOEs do not consider reputation building as the ultimate communication goal, but only focus on temporary or single communication tasks, without integrating long-term, public-oriented reputation building goals into their strategic planning.

Looking at the communication function, this book finds that neither CCA nor CRRC has established a dedicated communications department. CCA integrated the communications function into the chairman's office, and CRRC only recruited a crisis communications team. In addition, Chinese SOEs mainly focus on press releases, facts clarification and product promotion when communicating to the public, while lacking innovative expressions of corporate philosophy and corporate stories.

In conclusion, due to the lack of strategic planning, Chinese SOEs do not consider reputation building as a core corporate goal and do not develop a stable and comprehensive reputation signal delivery system.

6.2 A Re-examination of the Elements of Overseas Reputation Building for Chinese SOEs

Based on the theory of total corporate communications, this book points out that corporate reputation building is influenced by three levels of communication activities, including corporate reputation building behavior as primary communication, corporate communication strategy as secondary communication, and impact of media coverage as tertiary communication. At the same time, the book notes that the institutional environment in which the company operates is the context for all corporate communication activities to take place.

Following this line of thought, the book develops a study of Chinese SOEs in the U.S., attempting to explain how Chinese SOEs deliver reputation signals to stakeholders through primary and secondary communication activities in a particular institutional environment. It also seeks to examine the impact of tertiary communication, mainly media coverage, on the reputation of SOEs and how SOEs responded to it. Based on the previous theoretical studies and case studies, this book further refines the elements of reputation building for overseas Chinese SOEs.

6.2.1 Primary Communication: Three-Dimensional Reputation Building Behaviors of Overseas Chinese SOEs

Inspired by Habermas' three worlds logic, this book subdivides the reputation-constructing behaviors of firms in the subjective, objective, and social worlds into three dimensions: identity positioning, competence building, and ethics establishing. The reputation building behaviors of companies in these three dimensions are their primary communication, which directly affect the accumulation of reputation capital of companies.

6.2.1.1 Globalization and Localization: Identity Positioning of Chinese SOEs Overseas

Corporate identity means how a company defines "who we are". It is the starting point of corporate reputation building and the internal driver of corporate self-expression. Based on studies of Asian, North American and European companies, Alden (1999) pointed out that the corporate positioning strategy may be local, foreign or global. In this book, two Chinese SOEs are positioned with different identities.

CRRC chooses a local positioning strategy where the company focuses on "maximizing local value" and localizes production, purchasing, employment, management, and R&D to create economic value for the local community. While CCA's corporate identity is a mix of global standardization and local relevance. The company refines its local development strategy under the framework of the Group's global brand planning, so that the main brand and sub-brands can support each other and attempting to seek a convergence of global and local identity.

It should be noted that identity is the self-recognition and self-presentation of the company, which requires constant adaptation to the external environment. Symbolic interaction theory suggests that the self develops through social activities and interactions (Mead, 2012). Swann proposed identity negotiation theory based on this, suggesting that social members will observe their own behavior, the situations they are in, and the reactions of others to their behavior, to negotiate their own identity (Swann, 1987). For overseas Chinese SOEs, external public opinion is continually interpreting the identity of SOEs, sometimes resulting in conflicts between their subjective positioning and objective impression, which requires SOEs to adjust their identity.

In this book, the U.S. government and media generally highlight the state-owned attribute and prominent position of Chinese SOEs, which implies that the business attribute of Chinese SOEs are not widely accepted. But at the same time, state-owned attribute is a natural attribute of Chinese SOEs, and they should not and cannot hide it. This book argues that the "global localization" positioning is a more reasonable path for Chinese SOEs to negotiate their identities. On the one hand, Chinese SOEs should compete in the market as independent global companies, emphasizing their advantages in global operations; on the other hand, SOEs should become corporate citizens who respect local culture, take local responsibilities, and integrate into local communities.

Multinational companies are meant to transcend national borders, so in order to integrate into the global economic system Chinese SOEs need to eliminate the nation-state ontological mindset (Zhao, 2011). Facing the labels of "economic threat" and "government tool" from western countries, Chinese SOEs should work harder to become "global citizens" and "local builders", which is more in line with the value of "human community with a shared future".

6.2.1.2 Competitive Advantage Accumulation: Capability Legitimacy of Overseas Chinese SOEs

Corporate competence is the basis for companies to gain competitive advantage in the product service market. Both SOEs in this study are actively building their competence. However, the book also finds that the competence of Chinese SOEs is hardly recognized by U.S. society in general. The U.S. government and media continue to construct a discourse of "securitization" of Chinese SOEs, emphasizing that they enjoy "government subsidies" and cannot compete fairly in the marketplace, and suspecting that they are controlled by the Chinese government which could threaten U.S. national security.

In fact, it is not only the United States that reacts strongly to the business development of Chinese SOEs; many countries are concerned about the active performance of Chinese SOEs abroad, viewing them as beneficiaries of "state capitalism" and believing that their entry will affect the fair competition of other companies (Tu &Zhou, 2015). Such an environment of public opinion also de-legitimizes the competence of Chinese SOEs.

In this regard, overseas Chinese SOEs need to first define and explain their competitive advantages rationally and demonstrate that their business competence is not dependent on national support. Resource-based theory suggests that a company's sustained competitiveness comes from resources that are valuable, scarce, and difficult to imitate (Barney et al, 2001), therefore, what Chinese SOEs need to highlight are the heterogeneous resources that the companies develop independently in overseas markets, and they can demonstrate their competence of R&D, product services and project management to the overseas public.

In addition, Chinese SOEs need to strengthen their degree of embeddedness in their overseas networks to establish their irreplaceability. In every market, companies have social ties of exchange and cooperation with other organizations, which constitute the organizational network in which they operate (Holmlund, 1997). There are interdependent power relationships between organizations, and the more intensive the relationships a company establishes with other organizations, the more powerful the company is in the network of relationships, the more other stakeholders depend on the company (Pfeffer and Salancik, 2003). For example, CRRC has accumulated a solid community reputation by purchasing local raw materials, hiring local workers, utilizing local supply chains, and supporting local disadvantaged businesses. CRRC forms reliable relationships with local stakeholders, who actively endorse the company when it goes through a crisis.

6.2.1.3 Meeting Ethical Expectations: The Levels of Social Responsibility Fulfilled by Overseas Chinese SOEs

There is a hierarchy of corporate fulfillment of social responsibility. Carroll's four-part definition of CSR was originally stated as follows: "Corporate social responsibility encompasses the economic, legal, ethical, and discretionary (philanthropic) expectations that society has of organizations at a given point in time" (Carroll 1998). This set of four responsibilities creates a foundation or infrastructure that helps to delineate in some detail and to frame or characterize the nature of businesses' responsibilities to the society of which it is a part. Yin (2012), on the other hand, argues that corporate responsibility can be divided into three levels: responsibility that must be taken, responsibility that should be taken and responsibility that is willing to be taken. In this book, corporate responsibility is considered to be at two levels: normative and ethical. The former means that the company meets the normative standards and the bottom line, while the latter means that the company can meet the broad ethical expectations of the society and actively seeking ethical recognition.

Currently, the fulfillment of social responsibility by Chinese SOEs in the U.S. mainly remains at the level of implementing normative standards, but lacks in developing sustainable and highly visible public welfare activities and social responsibility projects. In the 2018 White Paper on Overseas Communication of Chinese Enterprises, PR Newswire noted that when Chinese SOEs make press releases overseas, the topics focus on "new products/services" and "exhibition information", accounting for 28% and 24%, respectively, while the topic of "social responsibility" accounts for only 2% (Shao et al, 2018). Concerned about cost-benefit, Chinese SOEs tend to put great efforts into corporate compliance to ensure basic operational legitimacy, but due to insufficient professional staff and funding, they do little to innovate in fulfilling their responsibilities, which makes them miss opportunities to build public goodwill through public welfare activities.

In developed countries, the public and NGOs have high expectations of corporate social responsibility, and specialized and continuous public welfare projects are more likely to gain public support there (Wu, 2013). Therefore, on the basis of ensuring corporate compliance, Chinese SOEs should develop more featured social responsibility projects to win the favor of local publics.

6.2.2 Secondary Communication: Systematic Communication Decisions of Overseas Chinese SOEs

Corporate reputation building is a dynamic process. Companies can create reputation signals through reputation building behaviors, and in order to deliver the signals to stakeholders, companies need to develop long-lasting and systematic secondary communication strategies.

For Chinese SOEs, the first step is to establish an overall reputation-oriented communication goal. Corporate communication helps an organization to create distinctive and appealing images with its stakeholder groups, build a strong corporate brand, and develop reputation capital. To achieve those ends, all forms of communication must be orchestrated into a coherent whole (Brønn & Simcic, 2002). However, this study finds that overseas Chinese SOEs have not integrated long-term, proactive, public-facing reputation goals into their corporate strategies. SOEs should raise the priority of reputation building at the strategic level and establish a systematic communication project based on the accumulated reputation signals of the company.

Chinese SOEs also need to overcome the fragmentation of their communication functions. Scholars have defined three characteristics of ideal corporate communication functions. First, the communication department should be involved in the corporate strategy making process, and ideally, the head of communication could take a managerial role in the company (Grunig & Dozier, 2003; Foreman & Argenti, 2005). Second, for large companies, there may be multiple departments that perform communications functions, with personnel, marketing, and finance departments all sharing some of the communications tasks (Ha and Ferguson, 2015), but it is important for companies to have an overall head of communications to coordinate these departments and clarify what should be said and how it should be said. (Van Riel & Fombrun, 2007). Third, with the development of media technology, the functional scope of corporate communication is changing dynamically (Heath & Coombs, 2006), with social media engagement, multimedia production, search engine optimization, and opinion monitoring becoming the most important corporate communication practices, which requires companies to recruit skilled professionals (Swerling et al, 2014).

In addition to this, Chinese SOEs need to identify stakeholder priorities and communication sub-goals. Mitchell et al. (1997) developed a theory of stakeholder identification and salience by bringing together three important social science concepts to characterize stakeholders: power, legitimacy, and urgency, which they labeled stakeholder attributes. The central relationship in their theory was that the more attributes a stakeholder had, the greater its salience would be. Depending on the overlap of the three attributes, the stakeholders of a company can be classified into eight types (see Figure 6.1 below).

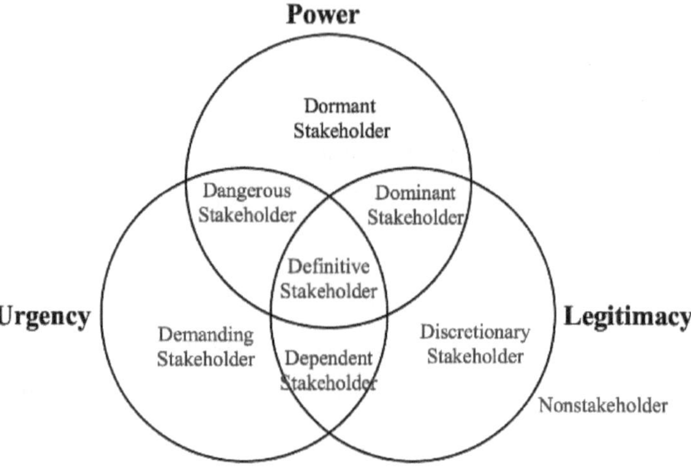

Figure 6.1 Salience Identification of Corporate Stakeholders

For overseas Chinese SOEs, the governments and media of their host countries are generally influential, so they are the dominant stakeholders of overseas SOEs. Chinese SOEs need to appropriately prioritize these types of stakeholders and pay more attention to maintaining relationships with them in order to avoid potential crises as much as possible.

Based on the identification of stakeholders, overseas Chinese SOEs need to further refine their target matrix. Communications that stimulate changes in knowledge, attitude and behavior are truly successful (Grunig and Hunt, 1984). Chinese SOEs can define different communication sub-goals based on the ways to change the "knowledge," "attitude," or "behavior" of specific stakeholders (see Table 6.2).

Table 6.2 Communication Sub-target
Matrix for Overseas Chinese SOEs

	Knowledge	Attitude	Behavior

Identity	Perception of SOEs' identity	Recognition of SOEs' identity	Express support for SOEs' identity
Competence	Perception of SOEs' competence	Recognition of SOEs' competence	Purchase of products and services from SOEs
Ethics	Perception of SOEs' Ethics	Recognition of SOEs' ethics	Participate in the ethics building activities of SOEs

Finally, for different stakeholders and communication sub-goals, SOEs need to choose the appropriate form of communication to achieve the intended purpose. Chinese SOEs can contribute to the perception and recognition of the company by different stakeholders through marketing communication, internal communication and external PR. Ideally, building corporate reputation is the common starting point of all corporate communication activities, which guides the establishment and achievement of sub-goals.

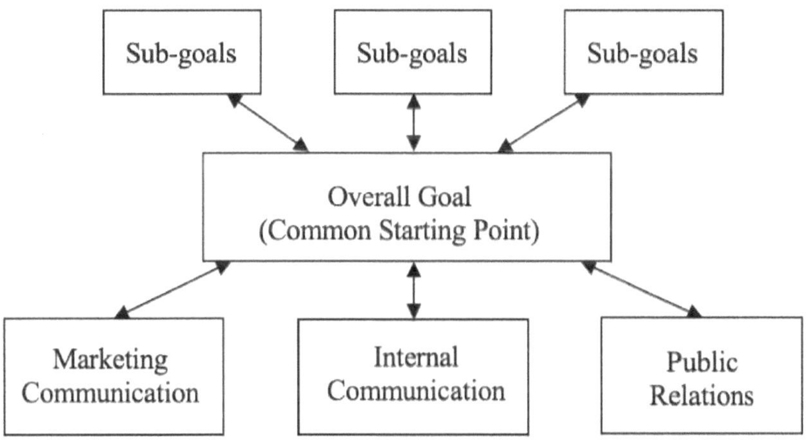

Figure 6.2 the Overall Goal and Sub-goals of Communication

6.2.3 Tertiary Communication: Image Refraction and Image Interaction of Overseas Chinese SOEs

Both the primary and the secondary level of communication are internal elements that affect the reputation building of overseas Chinese SOEs. However, the final formation of reputation is the result of different stakeholders decoding all corporate information they are exposed to. Therefore, the exploration of tertiary communication is necessary.

In his 1922 book, "Public Opinion", Lippmann (1922) argued that people do not know the world directly, but only as a "picture in their heads"; consequently, they responded to a "pseudo-environment" in their political judgments. This reveals the complex relationship between the media and social reality, where journalism is a product of social practice and a way of meaning construction with ideological tendencies.

For overseas Chinese SOEs, media reporting, as the most important third level of communication activity, is obviously influenced by the institutional environment of the host country. Numerous studies have confirmed that when a country implements a negative policy towards China, it will influence the media coverage and put Chinese companies in an unfavorable public opinion (Deng, 2019; Su, 2019).

By selectively reporting information and disseminating interpretations about organizations, news media exercise considerable influence on how organizations are known and made sense of by their external audiences (Deephouse, 2000; Rindova et al., 2007). Scholars generally refer to these externally produced representations of organizations and their actions as "refracted" images (Rindova, 1997), and have convincingly argued that the media and the images that they produce may serve as an important resource for reputation building (Deephouse, 2000). Carroll (2008) defined projected images as those emitted by an organization, which is the image that a company presents autonomously through its communication activities.

In the context of this book, the projected image of overseas Chinese SOEs is a collection of information conveyed through corporate behavior (primary communication) and corporate expression (secondary communication). While the refracted image of Chinese SOEs a collection of information produced by the media (tertiary communication), which is more or less influenced by the institutional power of the host country.

On the one hand, the projected images of overseas Chinese SOEs are usually different from the refracted images. On the other hand, overseas Chinese SOEs can try to intervene in the tertiary communication, making the projected image correct the refracted image. For example, in the case of CRRC in this study, government lobbying and media communication are used to correct the corporate image.

In fact, the projected and reflected images of overseas Chinese SOEs are in constant interaction and competition with each other. Each stakeholder will analyze all the corporate information they are exposed to and determine whether they feel "alignment of interest" with the company. The reputation dilemma of overseas Chinese SOEs boils down to the difficulty of making stakeholders form positive perceptions of them.

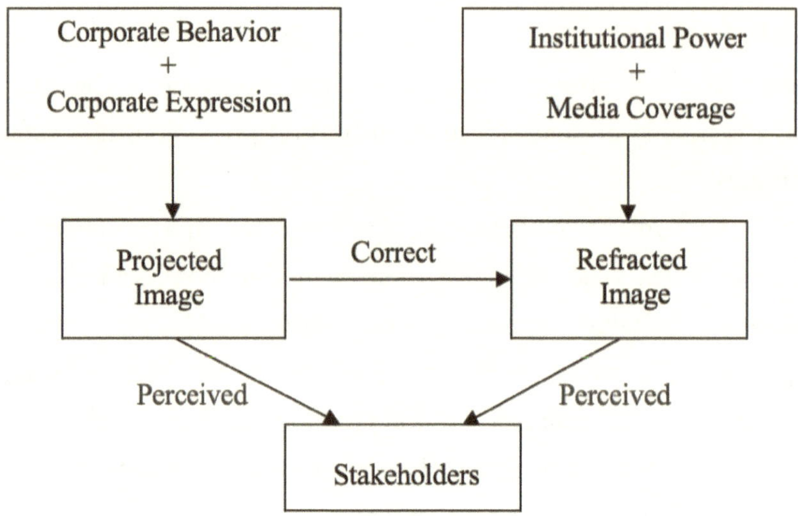

Figure 6.3 Interaction of Projected Image and Refracted Image

6.3 A Model of Overseas Reputation Building for Chinese SOEs

A model is a representation of an idea, an object or even a process or a system that is used to describe and explain phenomena that cannot be experienced directly. This book combines the disciplinary perspectives of communication and management to summarize the important elements that influence corporate reputation building. On this basis, case studies are conducted on two Chinese state-owned enterprises, China Construction America (CCA) and China Railway Rolling Stock Corporation America (CRRC America). Based on the findings, this paper attempts to propose a model of overseas reputation building for Chinese SOEs, with the aim of providing theoretical and practical references.

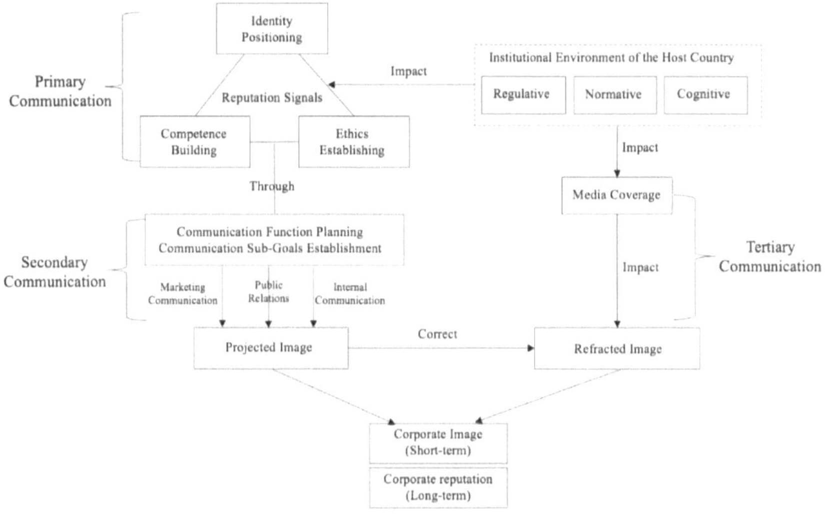

Figure 6.4 A Model of Overseas Reputation
Building for Chinese SOEs

First, in the process of reputation building of overseas Chinese SOEs, the institutional environment of the host country influences them in various forms. Therefore, scanning the institutional environment in which Chinese SOEs operate is a prerequisite for corporate reputation building. Regulative institutions are the political force that limit and regulate the behavior of SOEs in the host country, normative institutions are the moral expectation of the social role of SOEs, and cognitive institutions are the prevailing cultural value of the host country. Only by fully considering all institutional environment elements and clarifying the impact of different institutions on companies can Chinese SOEs conduct comprehensive and objective reputation building strategy.

After understanding the macro environment in which the companies are operating, Chinese SOEs need to position their identity according to their own conditions. A reasonable identity is to integrate globalization and localization, highlighting the advantages of Chinese SOEs' global operations while being adaptable to local values. Based on the identity positioning, SOEs need to build competence to provide material guarantees for business development. The legitimacy of SOEs' competence comes from their competitive advantages and their degree of embeddedness in the local organizational network; the higher the degree of embeddedness, the stronger the irreplaceability of the company. In addition, Chinese SOEs should also carry out social responsibility activities that are in line with their own identity to enhance stakeholders' moral recognition of the company. The reputation building behaviors of Chinese SOEs in the three dimensions should be mutually reinforcing, allowing companies to develop stable reputation signals.

The reputation signals of Chinese SOEs need to be delivered to stakeholders through reasonable and effective secondary communication activities. With reputation building as the ultimate goal and common starting point, Chinese SOEs should establish communication sub-goals and choose appropriate communication forms according to the goals. Internal communication is used primarily to disseminate information about corporate activities and build a shared understanding among employees about corporate goals. Marketing communications consist primarily of those forms of communication that support sales of products, services, and brands. Public relations is to communicate with the general public in ways that serve the interests of the company, it consists of numerous specialty areas that convey information about the company to the public, including sponsorships, events, media relations, and issues management. The ideal Chinese SOE's communication strategy would have the following abilities. First, the ability to coordinate all departments with a communications function to deliver a sustained voice in line with overall goals. Second, the ability to select appropriate forms of communication for different communication audiences. Third, the ability to properly plan short-, medium- and long-term communication activities, manage different communication sub-goals, and achieve long-term reputation goals in a step-by-step manner. Fourth, the ability to identify and resolve communication issues with stakeholders promptly.

Finally, as analyzed in the previous section, corporate behavior and corporate expression constitute the projected image of Chinese SOEs, while at the same time, the media, embedded in the institutional environment of the host country, are also creating the refracted image of Chinese SOEs. The two types of images constantly compete and interact with each other, influencing the perception of different stakeholders on the short-term images of Chinese SOEs, and the long-term accumulation of corporate images will eventually form the overseas reputation of Chinese SOEs.

Reputation research was born in the field of management, and most models of corporate reputation are based on a management perspective that views reputation building as a management process for companies. Fan Hong et al. (2018) have pointed out that there are currently six influential reputation models, including the F-A model, the M-W model, and the F-S model (Foreman and Argenti, 2005; Fombrun and Shanley, 1990; Mahon and Wartick, 2003). While these models generally emphasize the connection between corporate reputation and stakeholders, they rarely integrate communication activities into the reputation building process, and they rarely address the impact of the external environment on corporate reputation. The model proposed in this book integrates different disciplinary perspectives and provides a more complete and systematic research framework for the reputation building of Chinese SOEs, hoping to provide references for academic exploration and corporate practices.

7. Summary and Prospects

7.1 Suggestions for the Reputation Building of Chinese SOEs Overseas

Based on the case studies and theoretical discussions, this section will make further suggestions for the overseas reputation building of Chinese SOEs.

7.1.1 Establish a Reputation Evaluation System for Chinese SOEs

This study finds that overseas Chinese SOEs do not consider reputation building as a strategic goal for their business operation, which is due to their lack of willingness in reputation building. Overseas Chinese SOEs share a collective identity as "Chinese SOEs" despite being located in different industries and fields. To improve the overseas public perception of Chinese SOEs, they need to make reputation building as the strategic goal for their common development.

Chinese SOEs are managed by the State-owned Assets Supervision and Administration Commission (SASAC) of China. SASAC needs to place emphasis on construction of the overseas reputation of Chinese SOEs at the top level in order to better enhance China's national image. SASAC has revised its performance appraisal standards for Chinese SOEs several times, but it rarely included requirements for corporate reputation and communication effectiveness. In the latest version of the "Business Performance Assessment Measures for Heads of Chinese SOEs" released in March 2019, the document only mentions that Chinese SOEs should promote Chinese brands to go global, without proposing specific development paths and assessment criteria.

This book argues that SASAC need to incorporate reputation evaluation into the performance assessment of Chinese SOEs in order to guide them to make reputation building a strategic goal for corporate development. Based on theoretical studies and practical research, this section proposes a set of indicators for reputation evaluation of Chinese SOEs (see Table 7.1), in order to provide references for SASAC to develop a more reasonable reputation evaluation system.

Table 7.1 Indicators of Reputation Evaluation of Chinese SOEs

Dimension	Primary Indicators	Secondary Indicators
Corporate Identity	Corporate Vision	Goals, Mission, Values
	Corporate Design	Corporate Image System
	Corporate Management	Brand Management, Human Resource Management, Leaders Reputation Management

Corporate Competence	Operating Capability	Financial Performance, Product Quality, Market Share, Global Operations
	Innovation Capability	R&D Investment, Patent Quantity
	Talent Attractiveness	Highly Educated Talents, Professional and Technical Talents, Overseas Talents
Corporate Ethics	Legal Compliance	National Laws, Industry Norms, Technical Standards
	Ethical Responsibility	Social Welfare, Environmental Protection, Community Development
Corporate Communication System	Communication Function	Status of Communication Department, Number of Communication Staff, Investment in Communication Activities
	Communication Mechanism	Information Dissemination Mechanism, Crisis Management Mechanism, Public Opinion Monitoring Mechanism, External Cooperation Mechanism
	Communication Channels	Internal Communication Channels, Public Information Release Channels, Media Communication Channels, Marketing Promotion Channels

7.1.2 Adopt Multidimensional Reputation Building Behaviors

After establishing a reputation building strategy, each overseas Chinese SOE has to build its reputation according to its respective industry, target market, advantageous resources and cost-benefit.

In terms of identity positioning, first of all, Chinese SOEs should develop a brand philosophy that is suitable for global communication and allow the brand to adapt to the social culture and values of the host country. Secondly, Chinese SOEs should develop a localization operating strategy and incorporate the "local builder" trait into their identity to establish the legitimacy of their development. In addition, Chinese SOEs can hire more local managers, increase the proportion of local employees, or localize their brands through acquisitions and joint ventures.

With regard to competence building, Chinese SOEs need to highlight their strengths in global operations and independent science and technology innovation to prove their multinational management level and business capabilities. In particular, overseas Chinese SOEs can further enhance their local competitiveness by conducting technological research and development according to the local market demand.

When it comes to ethics establishing, this book finds that overseas Chinese SOEs invest more efforts in corporate compliance, but less in CSR activities. In this section, there are four key tactics for strategic planning that will help improve the outcomes of Chinese SOEs' CSR activities. First, link to company values. Chinese SOEs should align their CSR strategy with their brand, core competencies, and operational strategy, which will be different for every company. Second, get insights from various stakeholders. Chinese SOEs should develop strategic plans for CSR inspired by what customers, employees, and community members care about. Third, establish internal buy-in. Chinese SOEs will need their team's support, enthusiasm, and dedication to make the social responsibility program thrive. Hence, they should engage employees early in the strategy process by being responsive and inclusive. Fourth, Be clear and transparent. The CSR strategy of Chinese SOEs should include their plan for regularly and publicly discussing CSR initiatives—via website, social media, newsletters, email updates, reports, and even press releases.

7.1.3 Adjust the Corporate Communication Tactics

Corporate reputation is the comprehensive perception of all stakeholders about a company. This book argues that each stakeholder will form a judgment about Chinese SOEs based on the information they are exposed to, and that the essence of reputation building for Chinese SOEs is to make as many stakeholders as possible feel the "alignment of interests" with the company. In order to enable Chinese SOEs to better communicate with their stakeholders, this section proposes the following recommendations for the communication practices of overseas Chinese SOEs.

Overseas Chinese SOEs should set up specialized corporate communications department to coordinate all corporate communications activities. They also need to hire specialized talents according to the needs of overseas markets. At the same time, depending on the communication projects, Chinese SOEs should appropriately seek professional support from external teams. For example, cooperate with professional agencies in public opinion monitoring, media relationship management, multimedia content production and public service campaign project planning.

This study finds that negative reports on Chinese SOEs by overseas media have affected the public's impression of Chinese SOEs. Therefore, Chinese SOEs should establish a regular media communication mechanism to grasp the initiative of overseas communication, which includes the following. First, the information release mechanism. Chinese SOEs should regularly update their operations through websites and social media, and be able to make announcements through their own channels in the first instance when public opinion disputes occur. Second, opinion leader cooperation mechanism. Besides journalists, experts, scholars and commentators are important opinion leaders who can communicate with the public and guide public opinion, therefore Chinese SOEs need to form a good cooperation relationship with them. Third, public opinion response mechanism. Chinese SOEs should monitor public opinion in a timely manner and initiate contingency plans for unexpected public opinion issues.

PR Newswire published a report in 2019 showing that valuable news, industry perspectives and interesting stories were the most popular elements of business news for journalists. It is evident that when overseas Chinese SOEs release information to the public, they should be good at telling company stories in addition to basic factual disclosure. A company's story is a narrative about what it does, what it stands for, and what makes it exceptional. Great company stories are designed to inspire, creating a strong connection over time with customers and other audiences you want to influence and appeal to. To tell a good corporate story, Chinese SOEs should avoid grand narratives and instead tell everyday stories that can resonate with overseas publics to gain recognition from the international community.

Chinese SOEs tend to be involved in strategic industries such as communications, energy, transportation, and manufacturing, areas that are often regulated by local governments and make SOEs more vulnerable to national security controversies. Therefore, Chinese SOEs need to maintain close ties with local governments, for example, participating in social welfare programs organized by local governments and inviting local officials to corporate events. Moreover, when Chinese SOEs encounter controversies, they can also fight for their interests by conducting lobbying activities. In addition to governments, NGOs such as think tanks, trade unions, industry bodies, charities, and environmental groups all have different influences in various fields. As a result, it is important for Chinese SOEs to establish connections with NGOs in order to build bridges with the local community.

Chinese SOEs also need to focus on building social media matrix and embracing creativity business communication. Although most Chinese SOEs have created social media accounts, the activity level of their accounts is relatively low. Chinese SOEs need to better understand the content consumption habits of overseas audiences and produce content that is more in line with their preferences. Chinese SOEs should also differentiate their content production according to the positioning of different social media such as Twitter, Facebook, Instagram, YouTube, TikTok, etc. In particular, the global social media market has experienced a "video shift" in recent years, with short videos becoming the most popular online content. Luan (2017) proposes the concept of "visual persuasion", arguing that audiovisual language can maximize the "emotional involvement" mechanism in the communication process and reduce the cultural discount between countries. Chinese SOEs can try to attract more overseas publics through short videos.

7.2 Limitations of This Book and Future Research Prospects

Based on the intersection of communication and management, this study systematically analyzes the impact of three levels of communication activities on corporate reputation building. Through case studies on the reputation building of two Chinese SOEs in the U.S., this book summarizes their experiences and problems, and proposes a model for the overseas reputation building of Chinese

SOEs. However, due to the objective conditions, the study also has some limitations, which need to be overcome and improved in the future.

In the field of corporate communication and reputation research, theoretical exploration usually lags behind practical development. On the one hand, most practitioners are unable to condense their practice into theory from a macro perspective. On the other hand, researchers lack the opportunity to "immerse" themselves in the organization and are unable to obtain sufficient first-hand information, which can lead to slow progress in theoretical research. This book developed a new theoretical framework based on a combination of theoretical research and case studies, but there are still inevitable incompatibilities for real-life situations.

Besides, the large number of Chinese SOEs makes it difficult to be exhaustive when studying them. Currently, there are more than 10,000 Chinese SOEs operating overseas in more than 180 countries and regions in a wide range of industries. Although this book focuses on the U.S. market, which is the most strategic market for Chinese SOEs, it lacks in-depth research on other overseas markets due to time and objective constraints.

This book hopes that, based on the current study, the theoretical framework can be tested in more social contexts in the future, providing a more universal, scientific and comprehensive reference for the overseas development of Chinese SOEs.

The American writer James Russell Lowell once wrote in a poem that:

> *Reputation is only a candle,*
> *of wavering and uncertain flame,*
> *and easily blown out,*

but it is the light by which the world looks
for and finds merit.

Hopefully, the research in this book will inspire Chinese SOEs to truly understand and value reputation, and light up the road ahead in the process of "going global".

About the Author

Tian Xiangning, lecturer at the School of Television, Communication University of China.

She holds a doctorate in journalism and communication from Tsinghua University, and has been a visiting scholar at University of Colorado Boulder.

Her major research interests are global communication, corporate communication and media convergence. Her research has been published in various journals and conferences, including Modern Communication, Contemporary Communication, China Publishing, International Communication Association (ICA) Conference and International Association for Media and Communication Research (IAMCR) Conference.

Bibliography

Aaker D A, Joachimsthaler E. The brand relationship spectrum: The key to the brand architecture challenge. California management review, 2000, 42(4): 8-23.

Adi A. # CSR on Twitter: A hashtag oversimplifying a complex practice, Communicating Corporate Social Responsibility in the Digital Era. Routledge, 2017:340-357.

Albert S, Whetten D A. Organizational identity. Research in organizational behavior. Greenwich,1985: 263-295.

Alden D L, Steenkamp J-B E, BATRA R. Brand positioning through advertising in Asia, North America, and Europe: The role of global consumer culture. Journal of Marketing, 1999, 63(1): 75-87.

Allen F. Reputation and product quality. The RAND Journal of Economics,1984, 10:311-327.

Allison G T. Essence of Decision: Explaining the Cuban Missile Crisis. New York: Longman,1999.

Alvesson M., Willmott H. Strategic Management as Domination and Emancipation: From Planning and Process to Communication and Praxis. Bulletin De La Société De Pathologie Exotique 83.1(1990):82.

Anderson G, Arsenault N. Fundamentals of educational research. New York: Routledge, 2005.

Argenti P A, Howell R A, BECK K A. The strategic communication imperative. MIT Sloan management review, 2005, 46(3): 83-89.

Ashforth B E, Joshi M, Anand V, et al. Extending the expanded model of organizational identification to occupations. Journal of Applied Social Psychology, 2013, 43(12): 2426-2448.

Bai Yongxiu, Xu Hong. Research on Market Order and Corporate Reputation. Fujian Forum (Humanities and Social Sciences Edition), 2001,6:71-74.

Balmer J M, Gray E R. Corporate identity and corporate communications: creating a competitive advantage. Corporate Communications: An International Journal, 1999, 4(4):171-177.

Balmer J M, Greyser S A. Corporate marketing: apocalypse, advent and epiphany. Management Decision, 2009(5): 544-572.

Balmer J M, Greyser S A. Managing the multiple identities of the corporation. California management review, 2002, 44(3): 72-86.

Balmer J M. Corporate branding and connoisseurship. Journal of General Management, 1995, 21(1): 24-46.

Balmer J M. The BBC's corporate identity: myth, paradox and reality. Journal of General Management, 1994, 19(3): 33-49.

Balmer J M. The corporate identity, total corporate communications, stakeholders' attributed identities, identifications and behaviors continuum. European Journal of Marketing, 2017(9): 1472-1502.

Barney J, Wright M, JR. D J K. The resource-based view of the firm: Ten years after 1991. Journal of management, 2001, 27(6): 625-641.

Beauchamp T L, Bowie N E. Ethical Theory and Business, 3rd ed., N.J.: Prentice-Hall, 1980.

Berkowitz D, Adams D B. Information subsidy and agenda-building in local television news. Journalism Quarterly, 1990, 67(4): 723-731.

Berle JR A A. Corporate powers as powers in trust. Harvard Law Review, 1930, 44(7): 1049-1074.

Bernstein D. Company image and reality: A critique of corporate communications. New York: Holt, Rinehart and Winston, 1984.

Bhanugopan R, Fish A. Replacing expatriates with local managers: An exploratory investigation into obstacles to localization in a developing country. Human Resource Development International, 2007, 10(4): 365-381.

Blondel V D, Guillaume J-L, Lambiotte R, et al. Fast unfolding of communities in large networks. Journal of statistical mechanics: theory and experiment, 2008(10): P10008.

Bodnar K, Cohen J L. The b2b social media book: Become a marketing superstar by generating leads with blogging, LinkedIn, Twitter, Facebook, Email, and more. N.J.: John Wiley & Sons, 2011.

Brammer S, Millington A, Rayton B. The contribution of corporate social responsibility to organizational commitment. The International Journal of Human Resource Management, 2007, 18(10): 1701-1719.

Brønn P S. Corporate communication and the corporate brand. Corporate communication: a strategic approach to building reputation, 2002: 1-17.

Brown G, Brown G D, Brown G R, et al. Discourse analysis. Cambridge university press, 1983.

Brown T J, Dacin P A, Pratt M G, et al. Identity, intended image, construed image, and reputation: An interdisciplinary framework and suggested terminology. Journal of the academy of marketing science, 2006, 34(2): 99-106.

Burke E M. Corporate community relations: The principle of the neighbor of choice. Westport: Quorum Books, 1999.

Burke T. Risks and reputations: The economics of transaction costs. Corporate Communications: An International Journal, 1998, 3(1):5.

Buzan B, Wæver O, Wæver O, et al. Security: A new framework for analysis. Boulder: Lynne Rienner Publishers, 1998.

Cai Xiongshan. A Study on Barriers to Trade in Telecommunications and Internet Services in the United States. Information Security and Communication Privacy,2016(10): 81-87.

Campbell A, Alexander M. What's Wrong with Strategy? Harvard Business Review, 1997, 75(6): 42-50.

Cao Qiang, Wang Yingchun. Review of the "Asia-Pacific Rebalance" Strategy and Geopolitical Foresight in the Asia-Pacific. Journal of Eastern Frontier,2018,35(3): 61-67.

Cao Ran. Analysis of Media Construction Strategies for China's Image in the Context of "One Belt, One Road". Journal of Suzhou University of Science and Technology (Social Science Edition), 2018, 35(01): 99-106.

Carroll A B. The Four Faces of Corporate Citizenship. Business And Society Review, 1998, 100(1): 1-7.

Carroll C E, CARROLL C E. The Handbook of Communication and Corporate Reputation. N.J.: Wiley-Blackwell. 2013.

Carroll C E. How The Mass Media Influence Perceptions of Corporate Reputation: Exploring Agenda-Setting Effects

Within Business News Coverage [doctoral dissertation]. Austin: The University of Texas at Austin, 2004.

Carroll C. Corporate Reputation and The News Media: Agenda-Setting Within Business News Coverage in Developed, Emerging, And Frontier Markets. New York: Routledge. 2010: 137-148.

Caves R E, Porter M E. From Entry Barriers to Mobility Barriers: Conjectural Decisions and Contrived Deterrence to New Competition. Quarterly Journal of Economics, 1977, 91(5): 241-261.

Chen Ouyang, Jin Jie. Competition of Voices: A Study on the Involvement of Sources in Corporate Overseas Crisis Reporting. Foreign Communication, 2017(10): 37-40.

Chen Yang. Frame analysis: A theoretical concept in need of clarification. International Journalism, 2007(04): 19-23.

Christensen L T. Corporate communication: The challenge of transparency. Corporate Communications: An International Journal, 2002, 7(3):162-168.

Chu Shulong, Ying Chen. Individualism: The Dynamics of Development and the Causes of Problems in the United States. Contemporary World, 2012(09): 18-23.

Collier J, Esteban R. Corporate Social Responsibility and Employee Commitment. Business Ethics: A European Review, 2007, 16(1): 19-33.

Cook G. The Influence of National Cultural on American Business People – Managerial Implications for Central Europe. Central European Business Review, 2012, 1(2):46-51.

Coombs W T, Holladay S J. Unpacking the Halo Effect: Reputation and Crisis Management. Journal Of Communication Management, 2006, 10(2):123-137.

Cormode G, Krishnamurthy B. Key Differences Between Web 1.0 And Web 2.0. First Monday, 2008, 13(6):135-147.

Cornelissen J. Corporate Communications: A Guide to Theory and Practice, 3 Ed. London: Sage, 2011: 236-248.

Curran J, Iyengar S, Brink Lund A, et al. Media system, public knowledge and democracy: A comparative study. European journal of communication, 2009, 24(1): 5-26.

Dai Xin, Hu Yin Yi, Liu Li. How Chinese Fortune 500 Companies Conduct International Communication on the Internet - A Study Based on the Perspective of Website Design and Cultural Adaptation. Journalism and Communication Research, 2019, 26(004): 85-112+127.

Davies G, Chun R, Da Silva R V, et al. The personification metaphor as a measurement approach for corporate reputation. Corporate reputation review, 2001, 4(2): 113-127.

Davis K. Can Business Afford To Ignore Social Responsibilities?. California Management Review, 1960, 2(3):70-76.

Demchak C C, Shavitt Y. China's Maxim—Leave No Access Point Unexploited: The Hidden Story of China Telecom's BGP Hijacking. Military Cyber Affairs, 2018, 3(1): 7.

Deng Lin. A Study on the Image of China in Pakistani Mainstream English Newspapers under the Cultural Translation Perspective. Journal of Jiangxi University of Technology, 2019 40(06): 111-115.

Dennis T A, Talih M, Cole P M, et al. The Socialization of Autonomy and Relatedness Sequential Verbal Exchanges in Japanese and U.S. Mother—Preschooler Dyads. Journal of Cross-Cultural Psychology, 2007, 38(6):729-749.

Ding Donghong. Entrepreneurship. Beijing: Tsinghua University Press. 2017: 54.

Doane D, Vilaplana N. The myth of CSR. Stanford social innovation review. 2005, 3:22-29.

Doerfel M L. What constitutes semantic network analysis? A comparison of research and methodologies. Connections, 1998, 21(2): 16-26.

Doorley J, Garcia H F. Reputation management, Reputation Management. New York: Routledge, 2011: 30-63.

Dortok A. A Managerial look at the interaction between internal communication and corporate reputation. Corporate reputation review, 2006, 8(4): 322-338.

Dowling G R, Staelin R. A model of perceived risk and intended risk-handling activity. Journal of consumer research, 1994, 21(1): 119-134.

Dowling G, Moran P. Corporate reputations: built in or bolted on? California management review, 2012, 54(2): 25-42.

Dozier D M. Image, reputation and mass communication effects, Image und PR. Springer, 1993: 227-250.

Dozier D M. The organizational roles of communications and public relations practitioners. Excellence in public relations and communication management, 1992: 327-355.

Duncan T, Moriarty S. How integrated marketing communication's "touchpoints" can operationalize the service-dominant logic. The service-dominant logic of marketing: Dialog, debate, and directions, 2006: 236-249.

Duncan T. Principles of advertising & IMC. Journal of marketing Communications, 2005, 11(4): 309-310.

Eberl M, Schwaiger M. Corporate reputation: disentangling the effects on financial performance. European Journal of Marketing, 2005 39(7-8): 838-854.

Eberle D, Berens G, LI T. The impact of interactive corporate social responsibility communication on corporate reputation. Journal of Business Ethics, 2013, 118(4): 731-746.

Einwiller S A, Carroll C E, Korn K. Under what conditions do the news media influence corporate reputation? The roles of media dependency and need for orientation. Corporate reputation review, 2010, 12(4): 299-315.

Eisenegger M, Imhof K. The true, the good and the beautiful: Reputation management in the media society, Public relations research. Springer, 2008: 125-146.

Fairclough N. Discourse and Text: Linguistic and Intertextual Analysis Within discourse analysis. Discourse & Society, 1992, 3(2): 193-217.

Fairclough N. Language and Power. New York: Longman,1989: 26.

Fan Hong. Corporate PR Strategy Based on Social Responsibility. International Public Relations, 2009(02): 83-84.

Fan Hong. Multidimensional Shaping of National Image and Communication Strategy. Journal of Tsinghua University (Philosophy and Social Science Edition), 2013, 28(02): 141-152.

Fang Zheng. Research on the Construction of Corporate Reputation Measurement Index System in China. Journal of Shanxi University of Finance and Economics, 2008(30): 67-72.

Feagin J R, Orum A M, Sjoberg G. A case for the case study. North Carolina: UNC Press Books. 1991.

Fitzsimmons S R, Stamper C L. How societal culture influences friction in the employee–organization relationship. Human Resource Management Review, 2014, 24(1):80-94.

Fombrun C J, Gardberg N A, Sever J M. The Reputation Quotient SM: A multi-stakeholder measure of corporate reputation. Journal of brand management, 2000, 7(4): 241-255.

Fombrun C J, Rindova V. Who's tops and who decides? The social construction of corporate reputations. New York University, Stern School of Business, Working Paper, 1996: 5-13.

Fombrun C, Shanley M. What's in a name? Reputation building and corporate strategy. Academy of management Journal, 1990, 33(2): 233-258.

Fombrun C, Van Riel C. The reputational landscape. Corporate reputation review, 1997, 1(2): 1-16.

Fomburn C, Van Riel C B. Fame and Fortune: how successful companies build winning. New York: Financial Times Press, 2004.

Foreman J, Argenti P A. How corporate communication influences strategy implementation, reputation and the corporate brand: an exploratory qualitative study. Corporate reputation review, 2005, 8(3): 245-264.

Frederick W C. The Growing Concern Over Business Responsibility. California Management Review, 1960, 2(4):54-61.

Friedman M. The Social responsibility of business is to increase its profits, Corporate ethics and corporate governance. Springer, 2007: 173-178.

Gan Qin. Research Report on Corporate Reputation Management at Domestic and Overseas. Enterprise Civilization, 2005(05): 11-15.

Gandy O H. Beyond agenda setting: Information subsidies and public policy. New York: Ablex Publishing Corporation, 1982.

Ganguly B, Dash S B, Cyr D, et al. The effects of website design on purchase intention in online shopping: the mediating role of trust and the moderating role of culture. International Journal of Electronic Business, 2010, 8(4-5): 302-330.

Gibson D, Gonzales J L, Castanon J. The importance of reputation and the role of public relations. Public relations quarterly, 2006, 51: 15.

Giltin T. The whole world is watching: Mass media in the making and unmaking of the new left. New York: McGraw-Hill, 1980.

Goffman E. Frame analysis: An essay on the organization of experience. Cambridge: Harvard University Press, 1974.

Golan G. Inter-media agenda setting and global news coverage: Assessing the influence of the New York Times on three network television evening news programs. Journalism studies, 2006, 7(2): 323-333.

Goodman M B. Corporate communication: Theory and practice. New York: SUNY Press, 1994.

Gotsi M, Wilson A M. Corporate reputation: seeking a definition. Corporate Communications: An International Journal, 2001, 6: 24-30.

Granovetter M. Economic action and social structure: The problem of embeddedness. American journal of sociology, 1985, 91(3): 481-510.

Gray E R, Balmer J M. Managing corporate image and corporate reputation. Long range planning, 1998, 31(5): 695-702.

Grunig J E, Dozier D M. Excellent public relations and effective organizations: A study of communication management in three countries. New York: Routledge, 2003.

Grunig J E, Hunt T. Managing public relations. New York: Holt, Rinehart and Winston. 1984

Ha J H, Ferguson M A. Perception discrepancy of public relations functions and conflict among disciplines: South Korean public relations versus marketing professionals. Journal of Public Relations Research, 2015, 27(1): 1-21.

Habermas J. The theory of communicative action. Boston: Beacon press, 1984.

Hajer M A. The politics of environmental discourse: ecological modernization and the policy process. Science Technology and Human Values. 1998, 23(2): 245-8.

Hall r. The Strategic Analysis of Intangible Resources. Strategic Management Journal, 1992, 13(2): 135-144.

Hatch M J, Schultz M. Are the strategic stars aligned for your corporate brand. Harvard business review, 2001, 79(2): 128-134.

Hatch M J, Schultz M. Taking brand initiative: How companies can alignstrategy, culture, and identity through corporate branding. N.J.: John Wiley & Sons, 2008.

He Yang, Xu Jin. Changes in the Strategic Relationship between China and the United States and its Dynamics (2000-2017). Strategic Decision Research, 2019(10): 30-48+99-100.

Heath R L, Coombs W T. Today's public relations: An introduction. Thousand Oaks, California: Sage, 2006.

Hofstede G, Neuijen B, Ohayv D D, et al. Measuring organizational cultures: A qualitative and quantitative study across twenty cases. Administrative science quarterly, 1990, 35(2): 286-316.

Holmlund M. What are relationships in business networks? Management Decision, 1997, 35(4): 304-309.

Homans G C. Social behavior as exchange. American journal of sociology, 1958, 63: 597-606.

Hu Yu, Wang Shuaedong, Wang Jiajing. On Corporate Image: How to Become a Reputable Enterprise. Beijing: CITIC Publishing Group, 2019.

Hu Yu. Challenges of Image Communication of State-owned Enterprises. Economic Journal, 2017(08): 36-39.

Hu Yu. Image of Central Enterprises and National Image. China Soft Science, 2016(08): 170-174.

Huang Guoqun. Research on Corporate Reputation Shaping and Enhancement Based on Communication Perspective. Soft Science, 2009, 23(03): 94-98.

Huang Yinxia. Technical Regulations and Standards for U.S. Railroads. China Railway, 2006(12): 33-35.

Huo Bin, Zhou Yanhua. Research on the Relationship between Corporate Social Responsibility, Corporate Reputation and Corporate Performance, 2014(01):59-65.

Huse M, Neubaum D O, Gabrielsson J. Corporate innovation and competitive environment. The International Entrepreneurship and Management Journal, 2005, 1(3): 313-333.

Hutton J G, Goodman M B, Alexander J B, et al. Reputation management: the new face of corporate public relations? Public Relations Review, 2001, 27(3): 247-261.

Ihator A S. Corporate communication: reflections on twentieth century change. Corporate Communications: An International Journal, 2004, 9(3): 243-253.

Ismail M. Corporate Social Responsibility and its role in community development: An international perspective. Journal of International Social Research, 2009, 2(9): 200-209.

Jackson K T. Building reputational capital: Strategies for integrity and fair play that improve the bottom line. Oxford: Oxford University Press, 2004.

Jackson P C. Corporate communication for managers. Philadelphia: Trans-Atlantic Publications. 1987.

Jensen M C. Value maximization, stakeholder theory, and the corporate objective function. Business Ethics Quarterly, 2002: 235-256.

Joyner B E, Payne D. Evolution and implementation: A study of values, business ethics and corporate social responsibility. Journal of Business Ethics, 2002, 41: 297-311.

Kapelus P. Mining, corporate social responsibility and the" community": The case of Rio Tinto, Richards Bay Minerals and the Mbonambi. Journal of Business Ethics, 2002, 39: 275-296.

Kaptein M, Van Dalen J. The empirical assessment of corporate ethics: A case study. Journal of Business Ethics, 2000, 24(2): 95-114.

Kim D, Kim J-H, Nam Y. How does industry use social networking sites? An analysis of corporate dialogic uses of Facebook, Twitter, YouTube, and LinkedIn by industry type. Quality & Quantity, 2014, 48(5): 2605-2614.

Klewes J, Wreschniok R 2009. Reputation capital Building and maintaining trust in the 21st century, Reputation Capital. Springer: 1-8.

Kogut B, Singh H. The effect of national culture on the choice of entry mode. Journal of international business studies, 1988, 19(3): 411-432.

Lang Jinsong. Political Obedience: The First Choice of U.S. News Policy. Television Research, 2003(06): 23-25+21.

Lemke F, Clark M, Wilson H. Customer experience quality: an exploration in business and consumer contexts using repertory grid technique. Journal of the academy of marketing science, 2011, 39(6): 846-869.

Levitt T. Communications and industrial selling. Journal of Marketing, 1967, 31: 15-21.

LI Haiqin, Zhang Zigang. An Empirical Study on the Impact of CSR on Corporate Reputation and Customer Loyalty. Nankai Management Review, 2010(01): 90-98.

LI Xin'e, Peng Huagang. An Empirical Study on the Relationship between Corporate Social Responsibility Disclosure and Corporate Reputation. Economic System Reform, 2010(3): 74-76.

Li Zhi, Chang Xiao. On the Media Conservatism Bias in the U.S. Mainstream Newspaper Industry: A Textual Analysis of the New York Times and Wall Street Journal's Coverage of the Occupy Wall Street Movement. International Journalism, 2012, 34(08): 43-49.

Liao C, To P L, Shih M L. Website practices: A comparison between the top 1000 companies in the US and Taiwan. International journal of information management, 2006, 26(3): 196-211.

Lievrouw L A, Rogers E M, Lowe C U, et al. Triangulation as a research strategy for identifying invisible colleges among biomedical scientists. Social Networks, 1987, 9(3): 217-248.

Lin Jingxin. Reflections on the Reputation and CEO Image of Central Enterprises. International Public Relations, 2009(06): 46-47.

Lippmann W. Public opinion/by Walter Lippmann. New York: Harcourt, Brace and Company, c1922.

Liu Liang. Research on the Composition of Corporate Reputation and Measurement of its Drivers. Zhejiang University, 2005.

Liu Zhidan. Characteristics and Sources of Habermas' Lifeworld Theory. Journal of Central South University (Social Science Edition), 2014(03):149-153.

Lu V N, Plewa C, Ho J. Managing governmental business relationships: The impact of organizational culture difference and compatibility. Australasian Marketing Journal (AMJ), 2016: 93-100.

Luan Yimei. Visual Persuasion and National Image Construction: A New Audio-Visual Discourse in Foreign Communication. Journalism and Writing, 2017(08):14-18.

Luoma V. Corporate Reputation and the Theory of Social Capital. The Handbook of Communication and Corporate Reputation, 2015, 49: 279.

Mahon J F, Wartick S L. Dealing with stakeholders: How reputation, credibility and framing influence the game. Corporate reputation review, 2003, 6(1): 19-35.

Mahon J F. Corporate reputation: Research agenda using strategy and stakeholder literature. Business & Society, 2002, 41: 415-445.

Mahoney J S. Strategic communication: Principles and practice. Oxford: Oxford University Press, 2013.

Manfred S. Components and parameters of corporate reputation: An empirical study. Schmalenbach Business Review, 2004, 5(1): 46-72.

Mccombs M, Funk M. Shaping the agenda of local daily newspapers: A methodology merging the agenda setting and community structure perspectives. Mass Communication and Society, 2011, 14(6): 905-919.

Melewar T C, Karaosmanoglu E. Seven dimensions of corporate identity: A categorisation from the practitioners' perspectives. European Journal of Marketing, 2006, 40: 846-869.

Melewar T. Determinants of the corporate identity construct: a review of the literature. Journal of marketing Communications, 2003, 9(4): 195-220.

Melewar T. Facets of corporate identity, communication and reputation. New York: Routledge, 2008: 213-218.

Men L R. CEO credibility, perceived organizational reputation, and employee engagement. Public Relations Review, 2012, 38(1): 171-173.

Mirvis P. Employee engagement and CSR: Transactional, relational, and developmental approaches. California management review, 2012, 54(4): 93-117.

Mitchell R K, Agle B R, Wood D J. Toward a theory of stakeholder identification and salience: Defining the principle of who and what really counts. Academy of management review, 1997, 22: 853-886.

Nicholls J, LI F, Kranendonk C J, et al. Structural or cultural: An exploration into influences on consumers' shopping behavior of country specific factors versus retailing formats. Journal of Global Marketing, 2003, 16(4): 97-115.

Nielsen A E, Thomsen C. CSR communication in small and medium-sized enterprises. Corporate Communications: An International Journal. 2009, 14(2):176-189.

Noor K B M. Case study: A strategic research methodology. American journal of applied sciences, 2008, 5: 1602-1604.

O'brien F, Meadows M. Corporate visioning: a survey of UK practice. Journal of the operational research society, 2000, 51: 36-44.

Oliver S. Corporate communication: principles, techniques and strategies. London: Kogan Page Publishers, 1997.

Palmer J W, Griffith D A. An emerging model of Web site design for marketing. Communications of the ACM, 1998, 41(3): 44-52.

Parker C, Nielsen V L. Corporate compliance systems: Could they make any difference? Administration & Society, 2009, 41(1): 3-37.

Petty R E, Cacioppo J T, Goldman R. Personal involvement as a determinant of argument-based persuasion. Journal of personality and social psychology, 1981, 41: 847.

Pfeffer J, Salancik G R. The External Control of Organizations: A Resource Dependence Perspective. Social Science Electronic Publishing, 2003, 23(2): 123-133.

Pincus J D, Rayfield R E, Debonis J N. Transforming CEOs into chief communications officers. Public Relations Journal, 1991, 47: 22.

Pratt M G. Social Identity Dynamics in Modern Organizations: An Organizational Psychology. Social identity processes in organizational contexts, 2001: 13.

Ragas M W, Roberts M S. Agenda setting and agenda melding in an age of horizontal and vertical media: A new theoretical lens for virtual brand communities. Journalism & Mass Communication Quarterly, 2009, 86(1): 45-64.

Ragas M W. Issue and stakeholder intercandidate agenda setting among corporate information subsidies. Journalism & Mass Communication Quarterly, 2012, 89: 91-111.

Reese S D. The framing project: A bridging model for media research revisited. Journal of communication, 2007, 57(1): 148-154.

Rindova V P. Part VII: Managing Reputation: Pursuing Everyday Excellence: The image cascade and the formation of corporate reputations. Corporate reputation review. 1997, 1(2):188-194.

Robbins S S, STYLIANOU A C. Global corporate web sites: an empirical investigation of content and design. Information & Management, 2003, 40(3): 205-212.

Ruehl C H, Ingenhoff D. Communication management on social networking sites: Stakeholder motives and usage types of corporate Facebook, Twitter and YouTube pages. Journal of Communication Management, 2015, 19(3): 288-302.

Saxton M K. Where do reputations come from? Corporate reputation review, 1998, 1(4): 393-399.

Schilling M A. Toward a general modular systems theory and its application to interfirm product modularity. Academy of management review, 2000, 25(2): 312-334.

Schwaiger M. Components and parameters of corporate reputation—An empirical study. Schmalenbach Business Review, 2004, 5(1): 46-71.

Scott S M. Institutions and organizations. New York: Sage, 1995.

Shao Huadong, Li Xiaoyu, Zheng Meng. Research on Overseas Communication of Central Enterprises under the Perspective of Strategic Communication. Journal of Liaoning University (Philosophy and Social Science Edition), 2018, 46(04): 89-95.

Shaw E, Lam W, Carter S. The role of entrepreneurial capital in building service reputation. The Service Industries Journal, 2008, 28: 899-917.

Shim K, Yang S-U. The effect of bad reputation: The occurrence of crisis, corporate social responsibility, and perceptions of hypocrisy and attitudes toward a company. Public Relations Review, 2016, 42(1): 68-78.

Singh N, Matsuo H. Measuring cultural adaptation on the Web: a content analytic study of US and Japanese Web sites. Journal of Business Research, 2004, 57(8): 864-872.

Smidts A, Pruyn A T H, Van Riel C B. The impact of employee communication and perceived external prestige on organizational identification. Academy of management Journal, 2001, 44(5): 1051-1062.

Solomon R C. Ethics and excellence: Cooperation and integrity in business. Oxford: Oxford University Press, 1992.

Somers M R. The narrative constitution of identity: A relational and network approach. Theory and society, 1994, 23(5): 605-649.

Stuart H. Towards a definitive model of the corporate identity management process. Corporate Communications: An International Journal. 1999, 4(4): 200-207.

Swann W B. Identity negotiation: where two roads meet. Journal of personality and social psychology, 1987, 53: 1038.

Swerling J, Thorson K, Zerfass A. The role and status of communication practice in the USA and Europe. Journal of Communication Management, 2014, 18(1): 2-15.

Tian Zuhai. The Formation and Development of Modern Corporate Social Responsibility Theory in the United States. Journal of Wuhan University of Technology: Social Science Edition, 2005, 18(03): 346-350.

Tripsas M. Technology, identity, and inertia through the lens of "The Digital Photography Company". Organization science, 2009, 20(2): 441-460.

Van Noort G, Willemsen L M. Online damage control: The effects of proactive versus reactive webcare interventions in consumer-generated and brand-generated platforms. Journal of interactive marketing, 2012, 26(3): 131-140.

Van Riel C B, Fombrun C J. Essentials of corporate communication: Implementing practices for effective reputation management. New York: Routledge. 2007: 11+27+271.

Van Riel C B. Principles of corporate communication. N.J.: Prentice Hall. 1992.

Vendelø M T. Narrating corporate reputation: becoming legitimate through storytelling. International Studies of Management & Organization, 1998, 28(3): 120-137.

Wang Xinxin. Reputation management theory and its development. Economic Dynamics, 1998(2): 53-56.

Wang Yangcheng. Research on Talent Attractiveness and its Quantitative Evaluation. Industrial Technology Economics, 2006, 25(12): 115-119.

Wang Zexia, Yang Zhong. Interpreting and Thinking about the Three-Dimensional Model of Fairclough Discourse. Foreign Language Research, 2008(03): 9-13.

Wartick S L. The relationship between intense media exposure and change in corporate reputation. Business & Society, 1992, 31(1): 33-49.

Weaver G R, Treviño L K, Cochran P L. Corporate ethics practices in the mid-1990's: An empirical study of the Fortune 1000. Journal of Business Ethics, 1999, 18(3): 283-294.

Weigelt K, Camerer C. Reputation and corporate strategy: A review of recent theory and applications. Strategic Management Journal, 1988, 9: 443-454.

Whetten D A, Mackey A. A social actor conception of organizational identity and its implications for the study of organizational reputation. Business & Society, 2002, 41(4): 393-414.

Wu Fei. The Origin and Evolution of the "China Threat Theory". Nanjing Social Science, 2015(09): 7-16.

Wu Xianming. Institutional Environment and Overseas Investment Entry Patterns of Chinese Enterprises. Economic Management, 2011, 33(04): 77-88.

Xu Jinfa. Corporate Soft Power and Reputation Management. Beijing: Social Science Literature Press, 2010.

Yin R K. Case study research: design and methods. New York: Sage, 2009.

Yoon E, Guffey H J, Kijewski V. The effects of information and company reputation on intentions to buy a business service. Journal of Business Research, 1993, 27: 215-228.

Yu Jinjin. A Review of Modern Western Reputation Theory. Contemporary Finance and Economics, 2003(11): 18-22.

Zhao Kejin. Building the Future: An Institutional Interpretation of Congressional Lobbying in the United States. Shanghai: Fudan University Press, 2005.

Zhao Yuezhi. Communication and Society: Political Economy and Cultural Analysis. Beijing: Communication University of China Press, 2011.

Zheng Baowei, Liu Xinli. Research on News Values in Different Cultural Contexts. Media Today, 2010(08): 32-35.

Zhu Lanting, Yang Rong. R&D Inputs, Technological Innovation Outputs and International Competitiveness of Firms. Journal of Yunnan University of Finance and Economics, 2019(7): 105-112.